Stop Doubting Yourself

Overcome Your Limiting Beliefs, Face Your Fears and Build Unshakable Self-Confidence

MAX MASON

MAX MASON

this book has been derived from various sources. Please consult a licensed professional before attempting any techniques outlined in this book.

By reading this document, the reader agrees that under no circumstances is the author responsible for any losses, direct or indirect, which are incurred as a result of the use of the information contained within this document, including, but not limited to, — errors, omissions, or inaccuracies.

ISBN: 9798571682657

Your Free Gift

I'd like to offer you a gift as a way of saying thank you for purchasing this book. It's the eBook *Get Things Done: A Simple Guide to Overcoming Procrastination and Boosting Productivity.* You can get it by scanning the QR code below with your phone and joining our community.

SPECIAL BONUS!
Want this book for free?

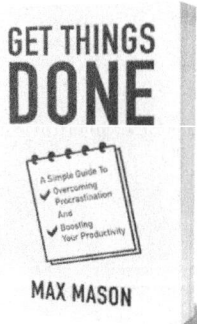

Get FREE unlimited access to it and all of my new books by joining our community!

Scan with your camera to join!

Contents

MAX MASON

Introduction

We all have an unbelievable power that influences people and leads to incredible transformations and achievements. It cannot be seen, touched, or smelled. It has no shape or form. Yet, it is what drives us to reach unimaginable heights and achieve incredible goals.

"So, what is this power?" - I suspect you're wondering. It is the power of belief.

Belief is what makes the impossible possible. It is the force that drives the most incredible achievements of mankind. Everything you see around you is the result of someone's thought. That thought was energized with the power of belief to make everything you could ever imagine real.

As great as the power of belief is, unfortunately it works both ways. While there are fundamental empowering beliefs that are a source of creation, there are also limiting beliefs that limit us in some ways and keep us from realizing our full potential and reaching our goals.

Our beliefs are formed from an early age from parents and other authority figures. Of course, not everyone has great supportive parents and teachers. Negative

11

experiences can lead to the formation of limiting beliefs that can sabotage your progress on the way to success in adult life.

Limiting beliefs are a source of self-doubt, a state most of us are so familiar with. Self-doubt is a crippling thought pattern that can lead to a vicious cycle of anxiety, depression, and procrastination.

The good news is, you can work with your thoughts and beliefs to eliminate limiting beliefs. You can replace your limiting beliefs with empowering fundamental beliefs. You can use your beliefs to transform your life.

When you overcome your limiting beliefs, they will no longer hold you back. You will be able to live the live you always wanted without getting crippled by negative thoughts. Furthermore, by replacing your limiting beliefs with new fundamental empowering beliefs, you will be able to boost your self-confidence and achieve great success in your life and career.

To do that, first in Chapter 1 we'll explore the nature and power of belief and its relationship with self-doubt and self-confidence. You'll learn how beliefs are formed, how they affect your life and how we can change them.

Then, in Chapter 2, you'll learn how to identify your limiting beliefs. We will establish what beliefs you have in general and which ones are limiting you in some ways. This way you'll be able to determine which beliefs are beneficial and should be kept, and which ones are limiting you and should be eliminated.

In Chapter 3, you'll discover how to initiate a mindset shift in order to overcome your limiting beliefs. You'll learn a simple yet effective step-by-step strategy that will help you replace your limiting beliefs with new empowering fundamental beliefs.

In Chapter 4, you'll find easy to understand, yet effective techniques and strategies that will help you move forward, increase your personal effectiveness, and maintain your newly found fundamental beliefs. While the hard work of identifying and eliminating your limiting beliefs is done, you have to maintain your new fundamental beliefs. You'll learn how to face your fears and introduce mindful movement routines into your daily life to relax your body and mind. Furthermore, you'll learn valuable techniques that will help you succeed in your life and career. Mindfulness will help you take a look at yourself from an observer point of view in order to determine what areas of your life need improvement. Responsibility will help you improve your personal effectiveness and become proactive in your responses to any circumstances. Acceptance will allow you to experience your feelings directly and avoid getting stuck in a vicious cycle of negative emotions, such as anxiety, depression, and procrastination. In addition to that, you'll discover how changing your environment can help you grow and transform your life. Lastly, you'll learn to accept discomfort, so that nothing can stop you on your way to success.

Finally, in Chapter 5, you'll discover the power of long-term thinking. It will help you focus on bigger long-term goals and prevent you from getting stuck in the moment because of temporary setbacks. You will also learn how to develop your emotional intelligence in order to master your emotions and use them to your advantage.

To keep expectations realistic, I am not suggesting that after reading this book you will never experience self-doubt again. Everyone struggles with self-doubt from time to time. After all, it is a part of human experience. It is completely normal.

However, I can say with confidence that by reading this book to the end, you will learn how to overcome your limiting beliefs and discover valuable tools that will help you overcome self-doubt, greatly improve your self-confidence and help you succeed in your life and career.

CHAPTER 1: Understanding the nature of belief

What is belief?

Have you ever wondered what belief actually is? It may sound simple, yet beliefs can be a difficult concept to grasp. Simply speaking, belief is an acceptance that something is true, especially without proof. It may sound a bit strange, but let's take a look at it from an evolutionary standpoint and discover what beliefs really are, and why it can often be so hard to change the existing beliefs.

Our brain uses beliefs to make sense of our complex world and navigate it in an efficient manner. Beliefs represent the concepts of how our brain expects things to work and how they should be related to each other. Our brain uses beliefs as templates for learning and conforms to the patterns formed by them.

Our brain has to make decisions about actions quickly. This may explain why beliefs are formed so quickly and often in the absence of evidence. Belief did not evolve to indicate truth, as belief is an unreliable guide to truth. It is more likely that the purpose of belief is to guide practical action.

This is why one person is able to believe in their goals and take action to make them a reality, while others are overwhelmed by self-doubt and have no will to press forward. The good news is, your beliefs do not represent reality. Moreover, it is possible to replace your limiting beliefs with new fundamental empowering beliefs. Now, let's take a look at what causes a person to form beliefs in the first place.

The causes of beliefs

There are many factors that may contribute to causing a person to form a particular belief. They can be divided into external and internal factors.

1) External factors include any input you receive from the external world through appraisal of evidence, acceptance of authority, acceptance of assertion, and the social dimension.

2) Internal factors include your previous experience, prior beliefs, and personality.

Let's take a closer look at these factors and how they affect the formation of your beliefs.

17

External factors

Most beliefs are formed during childhood. We learn them from an early age from our parents and other authority figures. Many beliefs are products of evolution - centuries and millennia of human culture. As children, we are inclined to believe our parents. And as adults, we tend to believe various authority figures.

Considering this, it's not a surprise our brain has evolved to readily accept and believe the things told to us, rather than to be skeptical. It makes sense from an evolutionary standpoint as a strategy for efficient learning from parents. It also promotes group cohesion, as humans are social species.

Charismatic persuasive individuals as well as compelling ideas can change people's beliefs. Sometimes it can be rational. But at times, it is not. People can often be easily influenced by charismatic leaders and social movements. It's especially true when they offer a stronger sense of validation and purpose, more powerful affiliation, or offer new self-identities and attachments than a person previously had in their life.

Internal factors

We experience the world surrounding us entirely through our senses. As a result, we find it hard to understand that these perceptions can sometimes be subjectively distorted and that they do not necessarily represent objective reality. People have a tendency to trust their physical senses and believe their perceptions even when they are hallucinating, no matter how distorted their perception might be. People always defend their perception of reality and try to explain away contradictions.

We give our subjective experience, our beliefs, too much credibility. We will always try to explain away anything that contradicts our beliefs. We will add layers on top of layers of distorted explanations instead of abandoning or restructuring mistaken beliefs.

Resistance to changing our beliefs comes from the fact that our beliefs are often linked to how we define ourselves as people - our identity. We want to feel that we are consistent, and that our behavior is aligned with our beliefs. We tend to rationalize our actions and beliefs in order to preserve the image of consistency, instead of admitting and accepting the fact that we are fundamentally wrong. It's embarrassing and at times can be quite costly in

19

many different ways.

How beliefs affect our lives

There is a variety of differences between the human world and the animal world. But there is one major difference that has a significant influence of our lives. We, as humans, need to make meanings of our actions and the events happening around us. Animals, on the contrary, function purely on instinct. For example, a dog doesn't care why he chewed a mat. And a cat has no need to understand why she likes to roll around in the sun. But humans have an inherent need to question everything: their behavior, the actions of others, and the world around them in general. We have a constant need to make meaning of our experiences, and this process starts from the moment we exist.

When we make meaning we come to conclusions. When we have made the same meaning several times about a repeated experience - this meaning then turns into a belief. This is especially true if the experience was traumatic or when we have no new or conflicting information to compare our meaning to. Furthermore, the less information we have, the more likely it is that our beliefs will be mistaken and probably rather limiting.

Beliefs create reality

Our brains have an interesting algorithm of sorting information. Events happening around us are always matched to our beliefs in order to help us make sense of life. Consequently, our brain is scanning every experience looking for anything that could possibly be matched to our existing beliefs. All the information our brain receives is scanned in search for anything that brings confirmation to our existing beliefs. When a match is found, the brain stores it and accepts it as truth. Other information that doesn't fit into the framework of existing beliefs is either distorted or discarded.

Limiting or mistaken beliefs are created, verified, and upheld in the same way as empowering or helpful beliefs. If you have a belief that you don't deserve happiness, then it will always seem like happiness is out of reach. Positive beliefs work in an opposite way, where life seems to be handing out good luck right, left, and center. Life is giving us what we believe, and our beliefs are creating good or bad luck by getting us to notice the things that match with our beliefs and discarding the rest. Our reality is created by our beliefs, so essentially, we are creating our own luck, happiness, and everything else.

For example, if you have a belief that you're not good enough, then every criticism, no matter how big or small, is immediately taken as absolute truth rather than just someone else's opinion. As a result, every mistake is then seen as evidence of being not good enough, rather than an opportunity to learn and improve.

The good news is that the brain works with positive beliefs in a similar manner. So, for example, if you have a positive belief that you are successful, the brain will search for anything that may fit in with that belief. Consequently, any positive affirmations such as "You can reach your goals" or "You can achieve success" will match up with your positive belief. Furthermore, any positive comments will also be recognized by the brain as a match. That's why it's so important to introduce and maintain positive fundamental beliefs.

Creation of a belief and matching

Let's take a look at how beliefs and matching work in more detail. Let's imagine there was a boy named Jack. Jack's mother had lots of pressure in her life, and as a result, she had little patience. She would shout at Jack repeatedly: "Look at what you've done!"; "Why on earth did you do it?"; "Can't you get anything right?". As adults, with our insight and experience, we can tell that Jack's mother was probably taking out her frustrations on the common mistakes any small child makes, as well as demonstrating her own lack of inner harmony or useful parenting skills. From an adult point of view, we can see a case of poor parenting and that Jack's mother is making a mistake.

Jack is a young boy, he's only three years old and he does not possess the knowledge available to adults. He can never think that his mother might be wrong. So, he makes what meaning he can from this experience. Jack could probably think, "Maybe I can't get anything right". After a few repetitions of such experiences, this meaning embeds itself into Jack's mind and becomes a belief. In this case, this belief is about Jack's identity because it includes the word "I" - "I can't get anything right". Beliefs can be about identity - "I can't"; or others' attitude - "People don't like me"; or the world around us - "It's a cruel world out there".

As soon as it becomes a belief, Jack's brain begins to match up other experiences to this existing belief. Furthermore, since Jack's mother most likely continues to demonstrate the same poor parenting practices, it becomes quite easy for the brain to find quick matches. And the brain doesn't stop there. It keeps looking for matches in any situation, so when other adults make comments or ask questions such as, "Jack, are you sure you want to play outside? Maybe we should stay home and watch some cartoons?", Jack's brain says, "There's one! They are saying you can't get anything right". If Jack sees someone looking at his sweater, his brain is likely to say, "There's one! They are thinking I can't get anything right! They are making fun of my sweater and how silly I look wearing it". In reality, the person is probably innocently thinking, "My nephew has a sweater like that". That example may seem a bit too vague for the brain to make a match like that; however, the brain is only looking for matches that can fit in with the existing belief, it is not searching for facts. And just like that, Jack's brain is constantly matching up his life experiences to his existing beliefs.

What happens when the brain is presented with information that doesn't match?

Any information that doesn't match the existing beliefs is simply discarded. The brain thinks, "That's not one", and dismisses it. Imagine for a moment someone with the belief "they are not good enough". When this person hears their friend praise them, "You've done a great job!", the brain has to discard this message because it doesn't match up with the existing belief. The brain says, "That's not one". That process is more often than not accompanied with thoughts looking for justification or excuses, such as, "That's not true, he doesn't really think that"; "He's just saying it to be nice, he doesn't mean it"; "He says so because he feels sorry for you"; "He said it this time, but that doesn't count because he normally doesn't do that". The brain can come up with a vast amount of reasons to show that the positive statement does not match the existing beliefs.

You can imagine the frustration experienced by those people who are genuinely giving positive comments to someone who does not believe they mean it. It's like talking to a wall.

Perhaps you even know someone who tends to interpret everything everyone says as something negative about them, and they won't ever believe the positive things people say and do. It's a truly frustrating experience. It happens because those positive things don't match up with their beliefs and their brain discards them as a result.

Beliefs can provide motivation to move forward or hold us back

All of us probably know a person who seem to have most things needed to live a successful life - intelligence, creativity, talent and humor, in some cases they may even have money. Despite all that, they never seem to get anywhere, so we often scratch our heads in confusion and wonder why such potential is never utilized. Nothing can stop us but our beliefs - when people have limiting beliefs, they are unable to push forward on their own. Instead they experience the old "Yes, but…" syndrome. "Yes, but I still can't do it".

On the other hand, all of us probably know a person who seems to have most counts lined up against them - lesser intelligence, lesser creativity, they may have poor health or a physical impairment and no money. However, when we see such an individual get ahead in life - we often scratch our heads in awe and wonder how a person with so many strikes against them could possibly accomplish so much. Nothing can stop us when we have positive empowering beliefs. When a person has positive beliefs, they can't be stopped by their own drawbacks.

Instead they experience the "Yes, but..." syndrome in reverse. "Yes, but I can do it despite all the problems that I have".

Negative feelings

People tend to think that their negative feelings are statements about reality or facts. However, it's important to remember that feeling is not a statement of fact, but of emotion. Experiencing your emotions does not equal accepting them as statements of fact about your own identity. Feelings are emotional reactions to beliefs.

If one feels inadequate, they can actively experience that feeling, realizing that even though they feel inadequate, this does not mean that they are inadequate in every aspect of life. It would be more appropriate to say, "I feel inadequate", rather than "I am inadequate", since negative feelings are not a statement of fact, but of emotion. What you feel does not represent your identity - it is only who you believe or think yourself to be at that moment. If one could suddenly dismiss all negative beliefs, what would remain is who they really are - a rather brilliant human being.

Most negative beliefs are created at an early age. As a result, we were unable to sort them through adult logic and reason. Consequently, we could not realize that we were accepting something that is not true and restricting.

Considering that feelings express emotional reactions to beliefs, we can turn our attention to negative feelings in order to discover our limiting beliefs. We can ask, "What belief can be matched up with those feelings?" or "What could possibly a person believe about themselves to generate such feelings?", "What does this feeling say about me?", "What meaning do I give that feeling?".

Negative feelings are often signposts to limiting beliefs. Once you discover your limiting beliefs, it is possible to remove them. Once limiting beliefs are removed, a person is finally free to be who they truly are. The person they could have been if limiting beliefs had not been created and engraved into their brain during childhood. The person free to explore and expand their own personal potential. The person you always wanted to be.

Changing your beliefs

Simply speaking, your beliefs are formed by the input you receive from the external world and how you interpret that input based on your internal convictions or inner self-talk. Consequently, it is possible to change your beliefs by:

1) Changing your internal convictions or your inner self-talk

2) Choosing your environment more carefully in order to change the external input

Now let's move on to discussing the nature of doubt, the source of self-doubt and how it can affect your life.

The nature of doubt

Although doubt is often regarded as the opposite of belief, it is not entirely true. Doubt is a mental state where the mind is suspended between two or more contradictory propositions, unable to be certain of any of them. Doubt on an emotional level is indecision between belief and disbelief.

According to a popular opinion, one has doubt if and only if one has less than the highest degree of confidence. However, lately another account of doubt has seen a rise in popularity: one has doubt if and only if one believes one might be wrong. Considering belief is a guide to taking practical action, this account of doubt directly correlates with the inability of some people to take action due to having doubts.

"If you hear a voice within you say "You cannot paint", then by all means paint, and that voice will be silenced" - the famous words often credited to Van Gogh.

It is fairly common to get into a sort of wrestling match with a little voice in your head that chips away at your confidence and dials up your doubts.

What if you mess up? You'll make a fool of yourself! What will people say? You're just not smart enough, capable enough, experienced enough, talented enough!

At some point, we all wonder whether or not we are doing enough, making enough money, or if we are going to be "successful" enough. This is a vicious cycle that can lead to crippling self-doubt.

The truth behind self-doubt

Self-doubt is a mental habit of questioning your own judgment or worth. By definition, individuals having self-doubt are uncertain whether their ability alone can lead to success.

Self-doubt, like all habits, can come from a variety of sources. And in fact, different people struggle with self-doubt in different ways - no two people's struggles with self-doubt are exactly the same.

Self-doubt often originates from one's childhood, usually as a result of the way they were raised. Consequently, self-doubt can become an issue later in adulthood, and in fact, it can accompany a person all their life.

It's important to remember that the factors that cause self-doubt initially are not always the same ones that are maintaining it now. For example, being bullied as a child causes a habit of self-doubt initially, but as an adult, the mental habit of asking other people for reassurance is what's maintaining it.

Limiting beliefs are created by our inner self-talk - our thoughts. Self-doubt is a crippling thought pattern that can deeply engrave itself into our brain. Nevertheless, we have to keep in mind self-doubt is a habit - nothing more. And no matter where it came from, it is always possible to free yourself from self-doubt by eliminating limiting beliefs and building better habits.

How self-doubt keeps you stuck

At one point or another, we question whether we are doing well enough or if we are capable of facing all the uncertainties that might come up as we grow older. We may experience feelings of self-doubt about our prior decisions and choices we made, or simply feel that we're not good enough.

The origin of self-doubt is often the lack of confidence or feeling that we are unable to do things that need to be done. Self-doubt is usually linked with uncertainty around things we can't control or worrying about things not going according to plan.

That being said, a certain level of self-doubt is actually healthy because it shows that you understand how you can improve in order to do a better job. However, a feeling of constant fear and self-doubt can have a massive negative impact on your life.

Let's take a look at an example:

John's boss has given him an important assignment because he thinks John is the most suitable person for the job. But instead of taking it as a recognition of his work performance, John starts to panic.

He panics about whether he is capable of delivering great results on that assignment. He is worried that he will make a fool of himself by failing to perform well. John spends time stressing over every single decision he has to make and pictures how things might go wrong.

As a result, fear will play a big role and will often lead to procrastination. Because of that people tend to delay their work and feel unmotivated.

Consequently, John hands in his work at the very last minute, and of course, he has the felling that he could do much better than this.

There are many reasons behind self-doubt. Let's take a closer look at some of them here:

1. Past experience and mistakes

Past experiences can play a big role in how we react to certain situations. That's especially true if you have had bad experiences before, like being in an abusive relationship or being fired without a valid reason. Our mental health can take a massive hit in such cases.

Past experience can influence our beliefs. However, it's important to remember you have to learn from mistakes and past experiences and not waste your time dwelling on them.

2. Childhood, upbringing and parenting

Most of our habits are shaped during childhood, and upbringing plays an important role in that.

Remember the story of Jack and his mother, who

33

constantly scolded him? If you were raised by parents who always told you that you were not good enough or you went to a school where students were judged heavily on their grades, it's not surprising you might have already developed the habit of questioning yourself.

 ### 3. Comparing yourself with others

It's fairly common for us to compare ourselves with others because we live in a competitive world.

We tend to compare our work performance with colleagues, we compare our achievements, our looks, and even our belongings to that of others, be it in real life or in the overwhelming world of social media. It's easy for us to envy the lives of other people and think that we are not doing good enough, or at least as well as they are.

When you're comparing yourself with others about what they have and what you lack, you'll start to lose yourself.

 ### 4. New challenges

It's pretty common to become overwhelmed by self-doubt when presented with new challenges because we have no experience on how to react or what things we need to do. The feeling of uncertainty and insecurity will naturally make you feel uncomfortable.

5. Fear of failure and fear of success

Even among successful people, previous success can become their biggest fear because they might think they've reached their peak, and this is the best they can deliver and that they will never produce anything that's equally as good.

With that being said, it's now time to take a look at confidence and its relationship with belief.

Confidence and belief

In short, confidence is a belief in oneself. It's the belief that one is capable of meeting life's challenges and succeeding - and has the willingness to act accordingly. In order to be confident, it's important to have a realistic sense of your capabilities and have a feeling of security in that knowledge.

Self-confidence is the conviction that you can trust your own judgment and abilities. It's the realization that you value yourself and feel worthy, regardless of any imperfections or of what others may think about you.

As mentioned previously, self-doubt is the result of limiting beliefs. Consequently, self-confidence is developed by building and maintaining fundamental empowering beliefs.

Self-confidence is important in every aspect of our lives; however, many people struggle to find it. Unfortunately, this can become a vicious cycle: people who lack self-confidence are naturally less likely to achieve the success that in turn could give them more confidence.

Self-confidence is the key to living a happy and fulfilling life. Let's take a look at some of the benefits self-confidence can bring. It might seem fairly obvious; however, understanding these benefits is an important first step on the way to living your best life with confidence.

Less fear and anxiety

The more confidence you have, the easier it will be for you to overcome your inner self-talk that says "I can't do it". You'll be able to dismiss your negative thoughts and do what needs to be done.

If you've experienced self-doubt, you probably know the rumination, or the tendency to mull over worries and possible mistakes, and constantly thinking about what could go wrong. Excessive rumination leads to anxiety and depression, and it can make us withdraw from the world. However, by replacing self-doubt with confidence, you'll be able to break the cycle of over-thinking and quiet your negative inner self-talk.

Greater motivation

Building confidence is done by taking small steps that leave a lasting sense of accomplishment. If you've ever mastered a skill, learned a language, improved your physique, or otherwise overcome setbacks to reach your goals, you're well on your way.

You might be thinking, what does that have to do with anything now? Yes, you were probably proud of that "A" in Math back in high school, but it doesn't really matter now, does it? If you look back on any significant accomplishment in your life, you will see that it took a lot of effort and perseverance to get there. If you could overcome setbacks and reach your goals then, you can do it now in other areas of your life where you feel self-doubt.

As your confidence grows, you'll find more motivation to expand your abilities. Of course, some negative "What if" thoughts may still arise: "What if I fail?" "What if I don't have what it takes?". But with an increased level of self-confidence, those thoughts will no longer limit you. Instead, you'll be able to just do it and act anyway, feeling energized as you progress pursuing the goals that are important to you.

More resilience ✗

Confidence provides the skills and methods to cope with setbacks and failure. Self-confidence doesn't guarantee you won't fail of course. But it gives you the conviction you can handle challenges and not be crippled by them. Even when something doesn't go according to plan and things don't turn out as expected, you'll be able to avoid dwelling on it and beating yourself up.

As you keep expanding your abilities and trying new things, you'll start to truly understand how you can learn from failure and mistakes. Moreover, by accepting failure as a part of life, you'll actually succeed more - simply because you will no longer have to wait for everything to be absolutely perfect before you can take action. The more opportunities you take, the more likely you are to succeed.

Improved relationships ✗

The more confidence you have, the less you are focused on yourself. It might seem counterintuitive, but it's true. People tend to think that others are constantly looking at them and judging them. In reality, people have their own worries and are wrapped up in their own thoughts most of the time. When you get out of your own head, you'll be able to genuinely engage with others.

You'll enjoy your interactions more because you won't be so worried about what others might think about you. You won't care what kind of impression you're making, and you will stop comparing yourself to others. Your relaxed state will help put others at ease and will allow you to build deeper connections.

Self-confidence can also help develop deeper empathy. When you're less focused on yourself, you're more likely to notice that, for example, your date appears to be a little down, or that your friend in the corner looks like they need a shoulder to cry on. When you're not drowning in your own self-doubt, you can be the person who reaches out to help others.

Stronger sense of your authentic self

Finally, confidence helps you find your true identity. With self-confidence you'll be able to accept your weaknesses and drawbacks, knowing they don't change your self-worth. You'll also be able to celebrate your strong points and use them more effectively.

Your actions will be aligned with your principles and values, giving you a greater sense of purpose. You'll be able to stand up and speak up for yourself. In other words, you'll be able to let out the best version of yourself. You're probably wondering how you can build self-confidence? The answer is quite simple - building self-confidence is a matter of changing your beliefs about yourself. But first, it is necessary to establish which beliefs are limiting you and need to be changed. So, let's move on to identifying your limiting beliefs.

CHAPTER 2: Identifying limiting beliefs

Before you can identify your limiting beliefs, it's necessary to establish what limiting beliefs actually are. A limiting belief is a state of mind, it's a conviction that you think to be true that limits you in some way. This limiting belief can be about you or your interactions with the outside world and other people.

Have you ever had thoughts like "I'm not good at dancing" or "I am so afraid of water, I will never learn how to swim"? These are examples of limiting beliefs that are holding you back and often falsely define you.

It's not a surprise limiting beliefs can have a variety of negative effects on you. They keep you from taking new opportunities, making good choices, expanding your abilities and reaching your full potential. All in all, limiting beliefs keep you stuck in a negative state of mind and prevent you from living your life to the fullest.

Causes of limiting beliefs

Now that you understand what limiting beliefs are,

41

it's time to take a look at what causes them. Let's see where they may come from and how they can influence your choices in life.

Some argue that people are inherently close-minded, as our inner biases cause us to only desire and accept positive and agreeable information.

Nevertheless, there are other things that cause limiting beliefs, apart from inner biases and our inherent inability to be open-minded. Here are a few you might resonate with, perhaps.

Family beliefs

Our parents have morals and values that they try to instill in us from an early age. They often originate from their own family beliefs and ideas about how you and the world should be. For example, it's things like what career paths you should take, how you should behave and engage with others.

Consequently, you can end up forming your own limiting beliefs based on the beliefs your parents tried to instill in you. For instance, your parents could reinforce a belief that authority should never be challenged.

As a result, you will believe that unfair treatment

from people of authority is something that has to be accepted and never opposed or challenged. You may even be unable to recognize this behavior, considering it to be the norm.

Education

Education contributes to the formation of limiting beliefs too. No matter who you're learning from: family, teachers, or friends - they all have an impact on what you accept as truth. This is because they're in a position of authority and they constantly convey information, ideas, and beliefs about how the world works.

When you're learning from such authority figures whom you respect, you are naturally more inclined to believe the things they teach you and accept them as true.

Experiences

Whenever you make decisions, it is natural for you to draw conclusions afterward. If, for instance, you fall in love and it ends in a heartbreak, you will probably conclude that love always doesn't end well.

These kinds of negative experiences can play a big role in shaping your limiting beliefs. It's important to remember that the conclusions you draw after negative experiences happen are only valid temporarily, and most likely they apply to this particular situation and not in general.

Faulty logic

When making decisions, we make so-called "return on investment" estimations. Quite often we easily conclude that the investment of time, effort, and money will be insufficient, and that chances of success are low and chances of failure are high. The return may even be negative as we could suffer losses or some sort of harm.

People make many mistaken decisions, often based on poor estimation of probabilities. We take a little data, sometimes without context, and apply it to everything. We mull over our decisions that are based more on subconscious hopes and fears than on reality.

Excuses

One of the reasons we use faulty logic and create limiting beliefs is to excuse ourselves from what we consider to be our failures.

When we do something and it does not work as

expected or at all, we tend to explain away our failure by forming and applying limiting beliefs that justify our actions and leave us blameless. But when doing so, we do not learn from mistakes and failures, finding excuses instead. And consequently, we can often chase ourselves into a corner, limiting our thought process and actions in the future.

Fear

Limiting beliefs are often driven by fear. Limiting beliefs are fueled by the fear that if we go against them, we or someone else can be harmed in some way.

Our decisions often have a strong social component and the thought of criticism, ridicule or rejection by others is sufficient to severely limit us. We also fear that we may be harmed due to carelessness or by others, and so we avoid doing certain things and interacting with some people or we may seek to appease them.

With that being said, let's take a look at some practical examples of limiting beliefs.

Examples of limiting beliefs

Limiting beliefs are the thoughts or convictions deeply instilled in your brain that hold you back in some way. These beliefs make you avoid doing certain things. As a result, they limit you in different aspects of your life. Limiting beliefs are the stories you tell yourself to justify playing things safe and holding back in the face of fear.

Before we move on to identifying limiting beliefs, let's look at some practical examples. Perhaps you can relate to some of them.

1. I am not _____ enough

Good, rich, athletic, tall, attractive, successful, no matter how you fill in that blank, it's limiting you in some way. Perhaps you see great job openings, but you don't even bother to apply because you think you're not good enough. Or you think you're not successful enough to associate with a certain group of people, so you keep on walking whenever you see them. Or you can't start getting in shape because you think you're not athletic enough, so it's pointless to even start.

These limiting beliefs about your worth prevent you from doing things you want to do. Let's say you see a group of runners on a Saturday morning or young people skateboarding in the park. You probably think you could never do that. This inner self-talk is caused by limiting beliefs. This negative self-talk is what prevents you from taking action and making things a reality in many areas of your life.

2. I am a _____

We often tend to define ourselves by our profession, which in turn dictates what we are and what we aren't. For instance, you may think: I'm an HR specialist, which equates to: I am not an advertising executive, so I shouldn't think about that area of the business.

Just imagine how limiting yourself in this way could prevent you from expanding your abilities, which in turn often leads to selling yourself short. We often limit ourselves without even considering that we all can have multiple talents. When you focus only on your primary area of expertise, you are neglecting other areas in which you have strengths and could potentially become quite successful. All this belief does is limit your professional growth.

3. I can't _____

This is one of the most common limiting beliefs, especially for people who don't have the growth mindset.

You aren't used to doing something, so you dismiss it because it's "not your thing".

Nevertheless, while you may think you can't dance, sing or speak in front of an audience, first consider how much effort you have put forth in trying. Considering you already believe you can't do these things, then I would guess not a lot.

"Whether you think you can, or you think you can't - you're right" - as Henry Ford famously said.

There can be a lot of things you don't know how to do, but if you aren't willing to learn, you're limiting yourself from exploring your full potential. Just think how your life would change if you could eliminate that belief.

4. I have to _____

As mentioned previously, parents try to instill their values and beliefs in you from an early age. Therefore, many people tend to live according to their family or cultural norms, values, and other potentially constraining rules. In some cultures marriages are arranged and decisions about how you live your life are made for you. For those of us who grew up in the Western world, these beliefs may seem extremely limiting. But for people from different cultures those practices are considered to be the norm, they often don't even give it a second thought.

Regardless of what background you come from, you probably have seen this limiting belief play out on a smaller scale. Have you ever thought how people around you would judge you if you acted like your real self and did not conform in some way?

For instance, let's say you grew up in a family where your parents and grandparents were doctors for several generations - a medical dynasty of sorts. It's expected that you will become a doctor as well after you graduate from your parents' alma mater. But what if your passion is to pursue a career in music instead? Your belief that you have to become a doctor because everyone was a doctor in your family for several generations will cause you to live a life of inauthenticity.

5. I don't have _____

- time
- money
- resources
- knowledge
- support

49

- motivation

Let's say, for example, you don't have enough money to go back to school. The tuition is expensive and everyday living costs have to be supported through a job or another source of income. Because of this, people sometimes don't even consider their options for going back to school and choose to stay at a job that they find unfulfilling.

Another common example of this limiting belief is thinking you don't have time to get in shape or work out. Maybe work is always busy or your children's schedules are packed and finding an hour to work out is a chore. This mindset is limiting because you're not allowing yourself to find time for yourself - your "me" time. You're thinking you don't have time for this, even though you never actually tried to free some time for yourself. Consequently, you are confining yourself to your current environment because it's the easy thing to do.

6. Other people don't like me

Our beliefs about other people and interactions with them can be just as limiting as our beliefs about ourselves. You may have found yourself in an unpleasant situation once in a social environment, and then you formed the belief that no one likes you. When in reality, people don't even really know you and haven't formed any sort of opinion about you.

But considering you already believe that people don't like you, you're probably not going to pursue friendships, partnerships or any sort of relationships with them in any way, which greatly inhibits your potential life experiences. This belief will also affect your self-worth in a negative way, especially if you believe that other people's opinions of you are more valuable than your own opinion of yourself.

7. I don't deserve it

This limiting belief can refer to pretty much anything: a raise, a promotion, or perhaps, you may think you don't deserve happiness in life. If you were often told that you didn't deserve things during your childhood when you were growing up, you may feel like you still don't deserve things in your adulthood. You may feel like you're not the "type" of person who deserves to be successful or have nice things. And this belief will certainly keep you down and prevent you from taking action to get the things you want.

This can further develop into another limiting belief that can be a massive obstacle to success. It's the belief that other people come first and your needs can wait. Like with everything else in life, it can be harmful to take this belief to the extreme on both ends, thinking you always go last or you always come first. But believing that you should be the one serving other people is a gigantic obstruction on your way to seeking success for yourself.

Believing that you don't deserve certain things in life will prevent you from aspiring to get what you want.

8. I'll get hurt if I fall in love

Having a fear of rejection often leads you to believe that getting hurt is inevitable, thus preventing you from being more open. Naturally, if you have experienced a painful breakup, you may believe that all relationships end this way. Moreover, if you have grown up in a broken home or seeing your parents fight a lot, it can make you believe that relationships are stressful and it's easier to just avoid them.

No matter what your beliefs are, prohibiting yourself to engage into any sort of romantic relationship will prevent you from sharing your life with another person and enjoying all of the good things that can come out of being in a relationship.

9. I shouldn't take away from other people

Some people believe that there is a limited amount of good in the world to go around. They think there is a limited amount of money, success, and happiness in the world to be divided among the entire world population. Consequently, some people believe that if we have more, then someone else will suffer from having less.

This is not true, of course, but if you believe it is, you will act in accordance with this belief. You won't take credit where credit is due and you won't strive to get the things you want. You will limit your success, your experiences, and your ability to live a fulfilling life.

These are just a few common examples of limiting beliefs. Perhaps you were able to relate to some of them. Now it's time to take a look at the limiting beliefs that are holding you back. Let's talk about the ways you can do some self-reflection and identify your limiting beliefs.

How to identify your limiting beliefs

There are a number of ways that can help you identify your limiting beliefs. Most of them require some personal reflection.

Before we move on to identifying limiting beliefs, first it is essential to figure out exactly what you want. Determine your goals and objectives you would like to achieve. It's possible you've been working toward these things for weeks, months, and even years, but for some reason you've been unable to achieve them.

It happens because you probably have a set of limiting beliefs that are holding you back. For now, let's not worry about these beliefs. First, it's important to clarify what it is you want. Ask yourself the following questions:

- What is it that I want?
- What goals do I want to achieve?
- What kind of person do I want to become?
- Why do I want all these things? What are the benefits?

The more reasons you find to achieve certain goals, the higher motivation you will have to push forward towards succeeding. And in order to change, you need to find the motivation needed to make this change first. Because of that, it's essential that you figure out exactly why you want to reach these goals and the benefits you will get from achieving them.

Before moving on, keep in mind that all beliefs are neutral. For instance, you may share a belief with another person. This belief might work for you in your situation; however, it will not work for the other person in their circumstances. Furthermore, a certain belief may work for you in one situation, but not in another. Thus, it depends on the situation and on the person holding that particular belief.

With that said, here is a step-by-step guide to identifying your limiting beliefs:

1. Identify your beliefs

In order to identify limiting beliefs, you have to find out what beliefs you have in general, and then determine which ones are limiting you in some way. Start by writing down your general beliefs.

Write down any beliefs you feel strongly about and that influence your daily life. You can sort them into different categories, such as family, relationships, career, finances, and health.

Once you've written down your general beliefs, take a closer look at each and every one of them and determine which ones are helping you grow and which could be limiting you.

When examining your beliefs, keep in mind how useful a belief is in your particular situation in relation to the goals that you are trying to achieve. If it assists and supports you in reaching those goals - then keep it. But if it doesn't help and hinders your progress - this is obviously a clear indication that you are dealing with a limiting belief.

2. Examine your behavior

Another strategy to identify limiting beliefs is to assess your behavior. Think about situations where you've acted in negative way and think why it happened the way it did. In many cases, if you examine toxic behaviors, you might discover that they are primarily caused by limiting beliefs.

For example, if you find it difficult to speak your mind after someone has offended you, you may have a limiting belief that conflict is bad. Which in turn could make you more close-minded and prevent you from having truly intimate relationships, as you're unable to open up and speak your mind and have healthy confrontations.

Limiting beliefs can often hide beyond conscious awareness. Nevertheless, there are key signals which can provide you with the clues you need to identify these limiting beliefs. These key signals become evident when you confront obstacles and challenges on the way toward your goals.

It's not surprising that it becomes incredibly difficult and, in some cases, impossible to overcome obstacles and problems when limiting beliefs are occupying the space in your head. For example, limiting beliefs can potentially manifest in the following ways:

- When you worry about making mistakes or the risk of failure
- When you worry for no apparent reason
- When you lean towards procrastination instead of getting things done
- When you make excuses
- When you complain about things
- When you make assumptions and/or jump to conclusions

- When you hesitate and/or have fears
- When you start dwelling on negative thoughts
- When you steer towards unhelpful habits
- When your inner voice speaks in limiting and unhelpful ways
- When you indulge in perfectionism, which prevents you from finishing or even starting some projects

3. Determine and write down the areas where you feel challenged

If you're constantly facing challenges in some areas of your life - the reason for that could be limiting beliefs.

Maybe you can't get a well-paid job or never had success in love. These challenges are often the product of limiting beliefs that you adopted and accepted them as truth.

As you're listing the areas where you feel challenged and the challenges you had to face, make a note which belief could be linked to these challenges. For instance, if you're always struggling to make enough money, examine your beliefs about money and how accessible it is to you.

Keeping these things in mind, write down all the limiting beliefs that come to mind as you work toward your goals. Beliefs that come to mind when just thinking about your goals apply too.

You could be thinking about a particular goal, and while thinking about it you may experience a sense of resistance. The stronger internal resistance you feel, the more limiting beliefs are lying dormant just below the surface of conscious awareness.

For example, you might have a goal to earn some extra money, let's say $10000 a year. But when you start thinking about it, you start experiencing a sense of uncertainty. This is exactly where you will find your limiting beliefs. You need to bring these limiting beliefs into conscious awareness. In order to do it, you should ask yourself these questions:

- What resistance am I feeling inside when I think about achieving this goal?
- Why can't I overcome the challenges to achieve my goal?
- What is holding me back?
- What exactly is getting in the way?
- What excuses do I have and why did I make them?
- What things do I complain about and blame others

for?

- Why specifically is this difficult and what is stopping me?
- What do I expect should happen and what happens in reality? Why is there a discrepancy here?
- What limiting beliefs are holding me back?
- How are these limiting beliefs keeping me from achieving my goals?

4. Acknowledge that these are beliefs, not truths

This step can be difficult, but it is the most important. You probably think your limitations are real. This is where you have to make a choice. Do you want to defend your limitations or reach your goals? Evelyn Waugh famously wrote, "When we argue for our limitations, we get to keep them". That is your choice, after all.

Remember that your limiting beliefs are assumptions you make about reality that are not necessarily true. They are often made in the absence of evidence and do not represent the truth. They are not helpful and do not assist you in reaching the goals you want to achieve.

Now that you've made a list of your limiting beliefs,

it's time to move on to shifting your mindset and overcoming limiting beliefs by replacing them with new fundamental empowering beliefs.

CHAPTER 3: Overcoming limiting beliefs

Your reality is created by your beliefs

A belief is a thought that we have thought many times over and over again - so much so that it has established the way we see ourselves and the way that we think other people see us.

When we think a thought for the first time - a new connection in our brain is created. It's weak at first, but when we keep on thinking the same thought over and over again, the connection gets stronger and stronger. This phenomenon in Neuroscience is called neuroplasticity, meaning that the physical structure of our brain actually changes as a result of the thoughts that we think.

It's important to remember that the original thought doesn't even have to be true for this to happen. Our brain naturally loves to be right, so once it has an idea, it will distort, discard, and generalize all the information it receives to build up and reinforce what it has already decided. We receive a vast amount of sensory input each and every day, so our brain has to filter the incoming information or it would become overloaded otherwise. Consequently, it sorts and selects the input that is in line with the existing beliefs and discards the rest.

We've discussed how poor upbringing and parenting can instill limiting beliefs at an early age. But let's imagine an opposite situation for a moment. What would happen if we had incredible supportive parents and teachers who gave us lots of positive input about ourselves? In this case, our beliefs can form an incredibly powerful platform for success and happiness. There is a lot of research on the growth mindset, which encompasses beliefs like these:

- I can learn anything if I put in effort.
- I have the ability and patience to see problems through and find a solution.
- I have the capability to bring the projects to completion.
- I can get along well with people.

But unfortunately, most of us have some kind of limiting beliefs, and as a result our negative inner self-talk can often sabotage our attempts to succeed.

When I was a kid, my teacher, whom I respected, once told me I should have more confidence in my abilities. He had the best intentions in mind; however, this had a totally opposite effect. It made me focus on the instances when I lacked self-confidence and ignore the times when I actually acted with confidence. Soon I started thinking I severely lacked self-confidence because my brain was focusing on all the information supporting this belief and discarded anything that proved the contrary.

Situations like this can lead to formation of limiting beliefs, and as a result, the negative self-talk that suddenly comes seemingly out of nowhere and starts telling you something negative about yourself. We've talked about some examples of limiting beliefs, but here are some more:

- I'm not smart enough.
- I'm not good at sports.
- I don't deserve it.
- People don't like me.
- I'm unlucky.
- I'm too young.
- I'm too old.
- I'm weird.

- I have a big nose.

Limiting beliefs can include any self-talk that starts with "you should", "you must", or "you ought to", or contains "always", "never", "people", "everybody", or "nobody". In this chapter, we will discover how to banish these limiting beliefs holding you back.

It's important to remember that no matter what beliefs we have accumulated during our lives, when we turn our attention to our beliefs and realize that they are not necessarily true, we can identify the limiting beliefs holding us back, isolate them and turn them around.

Before we move on to overcoming limiting beliefs, let's discover how to initiate a mindset shift in preparation to replacing your limiting beliefs with fundamental empowering beliefs.

How to initiate a mindset shift

A mindset is a collection of thoughts and beliefs that shape your thought habits. Because your limiting beliefs are triggers to negative feelings, changing your mindset is the first step on the way to eliminating the barriers that prevent you from achieving your goals and moving forward.

Here are the most important things to remember in order to initiate a mindset shift.

Understand that the decision is up to you

Have you ever started something like learning a skill or pursuing your goals, only to find your enthusiasm disappear soon after you just started? It usually happens when you realize the task is too difficult and the progress is too slow. No matter the reason, you have to remember the decision to feel stuck is up to you.

You have to eliminate your limiting beliefs and replace them with fundamental empowering beliefs, in order to control your life and move forward, achieve your goals and ultimately succeed. You can do this by taking that decision and telling yourself that you have the power to do it and acting according to that belief.

Remember that limiting beliefs are subjective and unreliable

No matter how strongly you believe something, it doesn't mean your limiting beliefs are true. They can be a comfortable excuse. But are you interested in defending your limiting beliefs or finding excuses instead of reaching your goals? Limiting beliefs can be useful and you may get some value out of them, as we are about to find out.

However, by definition these beliefs are limiting, and they inhibit your ability to achieve what you want and improve your life. Limiting beliefs are the reason people keep working jobs they hate and staying in toxic relationships. They keep your plans on the back burner and keep you down. They are the fuel for your negative self-talk. But you have to remember - they are beliefs, not facts.

With that in mind, let's move on to the step-by-step guide on how to overcome limiting beliefs and replace them with new fundamental empowering beliefs.

How to overcome limiting beliefs

1. Make a list of beliefs that are holding you back

We have discussed several ways you can use to identify your beliefs in general and limiting beliefs in particular. Now take a list of all your beliefs and examine it to identify the beliefs that have held you back. Let's say you imagine some things you would like to do or achieve, but you feel something holding you back. That usually points to limiting beliefs. Of course, there can be real hurdles in your way; however, many of them can be categorized as limiting beliefs.

One thing to keep in mind, in case you believe something has to be absolutely perfect before you can show it to the world - you can add perfectionism to the list. It's a common limiting belief that makes you concerned with achieving unattainable ideals or unrealistic goals.

You may find that the list of your limiting beliefs can get quite long, and that's okay. You have to write all of them down and then choose to focus on the ones you feel are limiting you the most. It will take quite a bit of work to deal with all the limiting beliefs, but once you've got the hang of this technique, it will come naturally to you.

Now that you've compiled a list of limiting beliefs - let's get to work.

2. Take one of your limiting beliefs and think of a time when it wasn't true

Despite the fact that limiting beliefs are often formed in the lack of evidence, once a belief is ingrained in your brain, it starts looking for evidence to support it. Therefore, we must find some evidence of the contrary - the counter-evidence.

You can think of it as a table where your belief is the tabletop and the table legs are the evidence. Once you find some counter-evidence - you remove one of the legs. The table will become wobbly and eventually fall over. This way you can destroy your limiting beliefs.

Let's say you lack self-confidence, which is a fairly common situation. You have to ask yourself: are there any situations you acted with confidence? It doesn't have to be something heroic for that matter. Maybe a stranger asked you for directions and you helped them. Or there was an emergency, and you did what had to be done before you even had time to think about it.

In case you can't think of an example, spend the rest of the day looking for evidence that might disprove your limiting belief. Look for the tiniest things that can make you doubt the accuracy of your belief.

If you can't find any counter-evidence - no need to worry. You can move on to the next step.

3. Examine how this belief has been holding you back

Write down all the ways you think this belief has

69

been holding you back - at work, in relationships, maybe it has even harmed your health.

The point of this is to let your subconscious know that this belief doesn't help at all, and the best way to do that is to associate as much pain with it as you can. So do your best and think of all the ways this belief has been keeping you from living your best life. Think of all the amazing things you could have achieved during the time you've been living with this belief. Feel the pain of all those lost opportunities and missed chances. Don't be afraid to make it hurt.

It can be cruel, but it's a necessary step to make your subconscious realize these beliefs aren't doing you any good in order to overcome them. Remember - no pain, no gain. It will all be worth it in the end.

4. Take a look at your past and try to find out when you first adopted this belief

It might seem like an unnecessary dwelling on the past, but it's important to establish how you adopted limiting beliefs in order to avoid repeating the same mistakes in the future.

It can happen in many different ways. It can be

something somebody said. Or an isolated incident that was generalized and you started accepting it as truth.

Try to remember what lead to the adoption of your limiting belief. Now think if there could be an alternative interpretation at the moment. You've associated a certain meaning with this missing belief. But were there any other meanings you could have chosen?

Let's say, someone said something mean or offensive to you. Maybe it was because they were having a bad day? Or they tried to correct your mistakes and overreacted in the heat of the moment?

Perhaps they did it to humiliate you? Was there something they had to gain by doing it? Was it someone you care about and whose opinion you respect? Were they living a fulfilling life or did they do it to compensate for something or just make them feel better about themselves? Perhaps this says more about them than about you?

Take a look at the situation from the outside. Imagine you were not yourself for a moment, but someone observing it. Would you still interpret the situation the same way you did? Would you still come to the same conclusions?

Try to think of alternative interpretations and write them down. Now replay the event from these different

71

perspectives. You should see how you could have attached a different meaning to this situation.

5. Think of the benefits you have gained from this limiting belief

It can be difficult and you have to be completely honest with yourself here. It's important to understand that limiting beliefs can sometimes serve a purpose.

Yes, they are usually used as excuses not to try things or get out of your comfort zone. "So how can they have any benefits?" - you might ask. After all, we want to get rid of this belief, don't we? So why are we looking for the reasons to keep it all of a sudden?

We're not going to keep this limiting belief, of course. We are doing it because it's important to find positive aspects in all things in life. This will help you figure out how you can appreciate your limiting beliefs and extract benefits from them in a different way once you've got them out of your life. We can look at limiting beliefs as mistakes of sorts, but we have to learn from our mistakes.

To do it, write down the feelings you associate with this belief - like comfort, security, lack of fear, avoidance of conflict, and so on. And now think of other ways you can

72

get those same feelings once this limiting belief is dealt with. Imagine how it would be if you could feel comfortable with discomfort. If you could feel secure with insecurity. If you no longer feared fear.

People naturally classify discomfort, insecurity, and fear as bad things that have to be avoided at all costs. That's because we attach such meaning to these things. Imagine what would happen if we could not get obsessed with avoiding them and just notice them? They would lose their power over us. It all depends on the meaning you give to certain things.

Keep this in mind and think how much time and energy you would save if you stop trying to avoid all the "bad" stuff. After all, it's neither good nor bad, it all depends on the meaning we attach to certain things.

As William Shakespeare famously wrote - "There is nothing either good or bad, but thinking makes it so".

6. Visualize removing this limiting belief

You've worked so hard to bring your limiting beliefs to the surface, and finally, it's time to remove them. But how exactly do you do it? It's not that hard, actually. You can do it with the power of visualizing.

73

Close your eyes and imagine yourself standing on a lovely sandy beach, looking out at the blue waters of the ocean. There are palm trees around you, and you can feel a gentle breeze. You're feeling calm. You're holding your limiting belief in your hand. Imagine it as a wooden tablet with words on it, for example.

Now you feel unbelievably powerful, infused with incredible energy. You feel immense strength coursing through your body. You're going to take that tablet and throw it as hard as you can. Put all the power, strength, and energy into throwing this tablet far into the ocean. And here it goes!

Look how far it's going! You've just broken a world record! It looks like it's gone at least a mile out to sea!

You observe the tablet flying through the air, as it flies further and becomes smaller and finally disappears over the horizon. Eventually, you see a tiny splash, almost too far away to notice, as it falls into the water and sinks beneath the waves without a trace.

7. Now think of a statement opposite to your limiting belief, write it down and say it out loud

It feels good, doesn't it? Now think of a statement opposite to your limiting belief - this will be your new fundamental empowering belief. Write it down and say it out loud. It might be a bit too much to start with, however. You can start with an interim belief and work your way up gradually.

For instance, if you're overweight, it's not entirely true to say "I'm slim and slender". You know it's not really so and your subconsciousness will know you're bluffing. In that case, you can start with "I have the willpower to lose weight and get that body I always wanted". This is definitely true! You can find a statement you believe in and work your way up from there. Make sure it feels positive, certain, and true to you.

Now close your eyes again and imagine living out this belief. Try to imagine as many details as possible. Live in this moment and feel what the new belief is bringing you - self-confidence, happiness and positive energy. Imagine this until it becomes as real as your surroundings.

75

For a moment, try going back to your limiting belief. Say it out loud. What feelings does it bring? Does it have power over you now? If you haven't completely gotten rid of your limiting belief - go through the last two steps again.

8. One belief being dealt with, now it's time to deal with all the others. Go back to step 2 and repeat for all your other limiting beliefs.

This process can take a toll and doesn't have to be done all in one session. You can come back to it later and do it over the course of several days or even weeks.

With all the limiting beliefs gone, it important to remember your newly found fundamental beliefs will need maintenance. You will need to do a routine check in order to preserve and maintain these beliefs. Negative thoughts and limiting beliefs can find their way back in at any point. Every few weeks examine your beliefs and make sure you're not letting any limiting beliefs back in. If you find any rusty patches, work on it until you are satisfied and it's all nice and shiny again. After all, your future depends on it.

Quick fix maintenance of your newly found fundamental beliefs

Here is a simple and effective exercise that will help you do a quick fix maintenance of your fundamental empowering beliefs in case some negative thoughts find their way back in.

If you find yourself dwelling on negative thoughts, try to shift your negative self-talk into the past tense. Let's say, you get a thought all of a sudden:

"I'm so lazy".

Change it to:

"I used to be lazy and indulge in procrastination, but now I schedule my tasks ahead and I am full of motivation. It's the first time in ages I'm feeling lazy".

This will reinforce the belief you are on the constant path of self-improvement, and limiting beliefs are fast becoming a thing of the past, leaving you free to move forward towards achieving your goals and fulfilling your dreams.

Once you've done this exercise, keep in mind you can do it in the moment for a quick fix.

Five empowering beliefs to replace your limiting beliefs

We've established how beliefs have power and influence on our lives. Our beliefs determine how we live our lives. We all desire a life that is fulfilling, nobody wants a miserable life languishing in mediocrity. People who lead successful and fulfilling lives have achieved this by choosing beliefs that support and empower them on their life journey.

You've learned how to replace your limiting beliefs with fundamental empowering beliefs. However, this is not everything there is to it. Just like you can adopt limiting beliefs, you can introduce empowering beliefs into your life without having to replace anything. After all, the decision is up to you. We all possess a wonderful power - the power of choice. It is a wonderful gift that enables us to make choices about what we want to believe and what we don't want to believe. Here are five empowering beliefs that will help you reach your goals and ultimately succeed.

1. My past failures do not define my future

If previous attempts at a difficult task led to failure -

don't let that define your future. The way out of this vicious circle is developing a growth mindset. It is the opposite of a fixed mindset, where you tell yourself that you are what you are and you can only do what you can do. For instance, "I've never been able to do public speaking, so it's pointless to even try". Growth mindset, on the contrary, encourages you to follow through until a positive outcome is reach. For example, "I will get better if I keep practicing".

Of course, practice takes time and you won't wake up a master public speaker if you just adopt this belief. However, it's the first and most important step on the way to constant self-improvement. I will help you move away from the feeling of being stuck towards success through constant practice and self-improvement.

2. I can handle anything that happens

Henry Ford famously said - "Whether you think you can or think you can't, you're right". This quote was mentioned previously, and it speaks volumes. If you think you can do something - you can. If you think you can't - chances are pretty good you'll never achieve your goals.

The belief that you can do something is what puts your mind and energy towards making efforts to achieve your goals. It is what gives you motivation and keeps you going no matter what. A positive outlook and belief in yourself can help overcome many negative, self-doubting thoughts that you might have about your work and career, your relationships, and ultimately your success.

In order to tell yourself that you can handle whatever happens, you have to truly believe that. To do it, you have to start taking small steps out of your comfort zone. Start stretching yourself a little. By building resilience one step a time, you'll be able to build unshakable confidence in your ability to overcome any obstacles on your way to success.

3. Failure is a wise teacher

Have you ever found yourself surprised when someone suggested you apply for a job or go for an opportunity that you never considered yourself? If so, you're not alone. 87% of people have experienced this, and nearly two thirds of them found themselves in this position more than once.

It's only natural to get a confidence boost from such offers; however, you might still find yourself thinking you'll never get that job when a great opportunity arises. What's usually behind such beliefs is the fear of failure.

Fear of failure is the main reason why people avoid tackling new challenges and remain stagnant in their lives. You have to realize that not getting something quite right on the first attempt just means that you can try again and do better. Remember, you've already found one way that didn't work, so now you can try a different approach.

In addition to that, people often fail to see what they can gain from the experience. It could be a useful insight into how things work that will allow you to prepare better next time. Furthermore, you can gain an understanding of the areas you need to improve in order to rise to the challenge in the future. So next time you don't get things quite right, focus on the process and how you can improve more, and less on the outcome.

4. Overcoming obstacles and dealing with challenges is the proof of success

Empowering beliefs are often based on embracing the unknown. They point to the possibilities and opportunities coming your way. Naturally, some of them will appear in the form of challenges and put your creativity and problem-solving skills to the test.

81

When you are determined to accept the challenge and do your best to succeed, you will find that you're no longer afraid of any obstacles or difficulties you may have to face on the way to success. Instead, you'll feel energized and ready to act.

Overcoming these challenges will help you move away from negative thinking. Instead of dwelling on negative thoughts, you will be able to see challenges as opportunities for growth. This shift in the perception of challenges is essential to succeed.

5. If something doesn't work - I will try something else

Sooner or later you may find yourself in a situation where no amount of planning or help of others could produce an ultimate failsafe solution. If something doesn't work, you can feel stuck, and it's natural. However, it's important to remember when to stick and when to quit.

You can feel paralyzed, the problem remains, and you can't move forward. In times like this, you need a massive dose of courage and a radical mindset switch. If you can't find a way to move forward, perhaps it's time to move on to something else. It might be difficult, considering how much time and effort you dedicated to get to where you are now, but you have to move forward no matter what. Being stuck doesn't help you pave your way to reaching your goals. If something doesn't work - remember what you've learned and move on to new opportunities.

Eliminating your limiting beliefs and introducing new fundamental empowering beliefs is just the beginning. Now it's time to move forward. Let's see how you can maintain your newly found beliefs and what useful practices can help you on the way to building unshakable self-confidence and living a fulfilling life.

CHAPTER 4: Moving forward

The most important step on your way to eliminating self-doubt is complete. You have identified the limiting beliefs that have been holding you back all this time and you've replaced them with new fundamental empowering beliefs. This is an essential part in our journey to building self-confidence and living the life you want. However, it's important to remember this is only the beginning.

You've done a great job - you've built a solid foundation upon which you can start building the new you. Of course, there are a lot of challenges ahead, but you will be able to overcome and learn from them with confidence and determination. It's vital to maintain your newly found fundamental beliefs. Here are some practices that will help you on your way to success.

Face your fears

Everything can be good in moderation and a little bit of fear is totally normal. After all, it prevents you from doing dangerous things and can help you choose safer options.

However, too much fear is never a good thing. You

could fear things that are not dangerous at all, public speaking being one of the most common cases. This, in turn, can prevent you from chasing some opportunities which could bring you great success. It can prevent you from advancing in your career or speaking openly in public, for example, saying a toast. Another example is the fear of travel. Perhaps you want to go on a vacation, but your fear of driving or flying prevents you from living the life you want. In case you feel that your fear keeps you down or creates bigger problems in your life, you have to learn how to cope with fear and ultimately overcome it by facing it.

There are a few things you can do in order to face your fears. First, you'll have to evaluate risks. Then you can create an action plan. This will help you stop avoiding your fears and face them instead. Nevertheless, first we need to establish whether it's necessary to face your fears, especially if they are not a part of your daily life.

Evaluate risks

Quite often fear comes from the lack of knowledge about the subject. Let's take the above-mentioned example of the fear of travel. Perhaps you're afraid of flying because you've heard about a number of in-flight incidents which resulted in injuries, or worse - death. However, statistics suggest that the probability of death on a U.S. commercial jet airline is 1 in 7 million. Compare that to the 1 in 600 chance to die from smoking and it doesn't seem so bad anymore, does it?

Furthermore, you can learn about the subject in more detail. For instance, you can learn what causes those bumps during turbulence. It's simply the movement of air masses having an effect on the airplane and slightly upsetting it. They pose a negligible threat to you, especially if you are buckled in properly.

There are less tangible fears, of course, such as the fear of public speaking, for example. Obviously, there are no statistics to support the evidence it's not as dangerous as it might seem. However, what you can do is simply practice. Learn about public speaking strategies and get inspired by successful public speaking ventures of other people. With practice and dedication, you will be able to improve your public speaking skills, which will make you feel more confident. With time and practice you will overcome the fear of public speaking.

It's important to keep in mind that if something feels scary, it doesn't necessarily mean that it's risky. You can overcome your fears by educating yourself on what risks are actually involved when doing things that scare you.

Create an action plan

When facing your fears, it's crucial to take one small step at a time. Going all in and doing something scary usually has an opposite effect, making you totally terrified.

It's important to be consistent when facing your fears. Having some anxiety is totally fine. You don't have to wait for your anxiety to vanish completely before taking action and moving forward. Otherwise, you can find yourself waiting for a change that is never going to happen.

Your action plan will help you stay consistent on your journey to facing your fears and overcoming them. It should consist of small gradual steps leading to you finally doing the things that you previously feared. Let's take the fear of public speaking as an example. Here is a sample action to facing this fear:

1) Stand in front of a mirror and give a two-minute talk.

2) Give a 15-minute speech in front of a mirror.

3) Record your speech and then watch or listen to it.

4) Practice giving a speech in front of your family member or your spouse.

5) Practice giving a speech in front of your family member and one friend.

6) Practice giving a speech in front of your family member and two or more friends.

7) Give a speech at a meeting at work.

Of course, there are things that are scary to practice. In this case, you can use imagined exposure. Let's look at the fear of flying an airplane as an example. It might be difficult to just get on a flight and fly somewhere, and there is no need to do so right from the start. With imagined exposure, you can start facing your fear by taking small steps, one at a time. You can induce a little anxiety by imagining getting on a plane. Just think how it would feel getting on a plane, taking a seat, buckling yourself in and taking off.

You can start watching videos about airplanes, flights, and travel. You can go to an area near an airport where you can watch planes take off and land. Learning more about planes and flight, as well as being near them, can help ease fear over time by getting used to things that you had feared before. With the latest developments in virtual reality, you may consider virtual reality treatment as an option to provide exposure therapy. It's been found to be quite effective in that regard.

Why it can be worse to avoid your fears

When you avoid your fears, you tell your brain you can't handle them. While in the short term avoiding the situations you fear can make you feel better and safer, it may cause increased anxiety in the long term. On the other hand, facing your fears step by step helps you decrease anxiety by making your brain getting used to fear. The brain has to face repeated exposure to fear in order to overcome it.

Is it necessary to face your fears?

Of course, it's not necessary to defeat every fear you might have. Some of them do not disrupt your daily life, such as the fear of tsunamis when you live a thousand miles away from the ocean. However, it can become a problem if you live near the coast. You can panic when you hear about incoming storms or earthquakes, as you think your life might be in danger. Or perhaps, you may avoid going on a vacation to coastal regions because of that fear.

Consider what your fears are preventing you from doing and establish whether it is a serious problem you have to confront. Are your fears keeping you from living a fulfilling life and doing what you want?

You can take a similar approach to tackling limiting beliefs. Write down your fears and consider the advantages and disadvantages of facing this fear. Then do the same for not facing this fear. Consider the things you can achieve and how your life would change if you overcome your fear. Taking this approach can help you establish what fears you have to face and which ones are not affecting your everyday life that much.

Fears and phobias

One important thing to keep in mind when establishing whether it is necessary to face your fears is the difference between a fear and a phobia. The key difference between them is the strength of fear response and its effect on your everyday life. Both fears and phobias cause an emotional response, but phobias cause a response that is so disproportionate to the threat that it affects your daily life in a negative and limiting way. It can often interfere with a person's ability to function.

Taking the fear of flying as an example, it can make you anxious about an upcoming flight or even make you consider different means of transport. But aerophobia, a phobia surrounding everything connected to flying, can affect your everyday life in far more dramatic ways.

For example, you can spend a massive amount of time worrying about flying, even though you don't have to fly anywhere in the near future. You can become scared of airports and even being near them. You can experience anxiety when planes fly overhead. Needless to say, you may be unable to board a flight at all. If you somehow board a plane, you can experience a strong psychological response that can include shaking, sweating, and crying. Treating phobias is a difficult process, and it can include elements of gradually facing the fear with the help of guided therapy. However, it can also include alternative therapies and even medication.

The best way to overcome your fears is to face them head-on; however, it's important to remember to take things one step at a time. This way you will be able to overcome and move past your fears instead of getting further traumatized by them.

Challenge your thoughts

A part of living with fears is having irrational thoughts that don't necessarily make sense. These thoughts are often of the worse-case scenario variety. You can find yourself caught in the vicious "what if" cycle, which can hold you back and prevent you from achieving a lot of things in your life.

There is one simple method to break out of this vicious cycle. When you experience such thoughts, stop and ask yourself the following questions:

- Is it really likely to happen?
- Is this a rational thought?
- Has this ever happened to me before?
- What's the worst that can actually happen? Can I handle that?

After going through these questions, you will be able to reframe your thinking. Let's say you are afraid to cross a bridge. Instead of thinking, "I won't cross that bridge, what if it suddenly starts falling apart and I will fall down?", change your thoughts to something like this: "Every day thousands of people cross that bridge. I will cross that bridge and everything will be fine".

Now that you know how to face your fears and whether it's necessary to face them in the first place, let's move on to another useful habit - mindful movement which will help you relax and calm your body and mind.

To calm your mind and body - get moving

Facing your fears is a great way to reduce anxiety and build more self-confidence. However, consistent self-improvement is the key to reaching your full potential. Let's see how mindful movement can help you relax and calm your mind and body to further reduce anxiety and stress.

A burst of physical activity helps burn off stress hormones, as designed by nature. Of course, you don't need to be under physical threat to use exercise as a way to reduce daily stress. You don't have to do any heavy exercise either, as any form of movement helps relive the muscle tension. It can be any activity like yoga, stretching, or any sort of repetitive movement, such as walking, running, swimming, cycling, or rowing. All of these activities help trigger a relaxation response, and they are especially useful if you do them regularly.

During exercise try to increase your awareness - notice what and how you're feeling, your environment and what happens around you. It helps increase the stress-relief benefits of any physical activity. This will help you become calmer and more focused. Such an approach is effective with any psychical activity, no matter whether it's a walk or strength training. Coordinate your breathing with rhythmic movement as you move your feet or raise and lower the weights, while keeping attention on the sensations in your body.

You should breathe rhythmically. Become aware how breathing complements your activity. Focusing on movement and breathing will help turn your mind away from disruptive negative thoughts.

Benefits of rhythmic movement

Most of us have experienced some kind of trauma or stress in the past. There is nothing wrong with it - it's a part of human life. Even if we haven't experienced any trauma, we live in a stressful world and it's easy to get overwhelmed. Because of that, we are often fatigued and experience excessive muscle tension. This, in turn, makes us feel anxious and exhausted.

It often happens that anxiety is the result of feeling stuck. The feeling of helplessness and the perceived inability to resolve or escape a difficult situation is a common occurrence in the modern lifestyle. Rhythmic movement is a great solution to get out of your head and get yourself unstuck.

Stress accumulates in our bodies over time, and we get used to this tension. We take it everywhere we go and it can have a big impact on our minds and bodies. Movement is a natural way to release this tension and return to a relaxed state. Rhythmic movement can trigger a mindful state and help reset your body by activating healing and renewal processes.

Rhythmic movement can be a therapeutic experience, as it brings your mind and body together, relaxes the nervous system and muscles, and allows your brain to activate the healing process. Furthermore, rhythmic movement is a grounding activity. Feeling grounded helps you deal with any worries or stress.

Considering that anxiety is the result of feeling stuck in your thoughts and being unable to resolve something, rhythmic movement helps you get out of your head. This, in turn, allows you to ground yourself and reconnect with your body in order to return to a relaxed and focused state. You will be able to tackle any problems head-on with increased energy and focus.

In addition to that, rhythmic movement improves your mood, reduces emotional stress and inflammation, and enhances your immune system. It makes you more relaxed, focused, and increases the feeling of security. It's exactly what we need in our daily struggles.

Five movement-based practices to relax your body and mind

There are a variety of activities apart from meditation that have a therapeutic effect and don't require you to sit still for twenty minutes. Any relaxing and repetitive movement can have a similar effect to meditation. All you have to do is go slowly and bring mindfulness to your movements. It's easier to include into your daily routine, since you enjoy it and it doesn't feel like a chore. Below you will find some of the most effective and accessible practices:

1. Walking

Walking is one of the easiest and most natural movement techniques. It helps you clear your head and release tension from your muscles and stress from your body.

The recipe for a mindful walk

Taking a mindful walk is a great example of exercising with relaxation in mind. "How does a mindful walk differ from a regular one?" - you are probably wondering. The main difference is expanding your awareness, both of your body and your surroundings. As you move and breathe rhythmically, start paying attention to the sensations of your body. Become aware of how the air flows into your nostrils and back into the atmosphere as you breathe.

Then gradually expand awareness to your surroundings. Pay attention to any sights and smells you encounter. Feel the smell of flowers, grass, trees, wet asphalt and anything that surrounds you. Notice how the wind blows over your body. Consider how the surface under your feet feels when you walk over it. Take a look at the thoughts moving through your mind. A slow, mindful walk helps you relax and gain focus.

Alternatively, a more energizing brisk walk can help you push your limits and relax at the same time. In this case, pay more attention to the sensations of your body, such as your heightened heart rate and faster breathing, and notice the way your muscles react when you push them harder.

2. Hatha yoga

97

Hatha yoga can be one of the most rewarding movement practices. It places emphasis on your breathing with addition of asana practice, which helps you trigger the state of mindfulness. It might sound a bit complicated, but in reality, it's rather simple and accessible to everyone. There is no need to join Yoga classes or hire a personal trainer. There are numerous instructional videos on YouTube, which you can use to start practicing Hatha Yoga at home.

3. Gardening

Gardening connects you to the nature like nothing else. It's a great therapeutic experience that helps you deal with anxiety and tame your mind when thoughts start running through it uncontrollably. It's a perfect activity to become mindful and engage with nature. It's a calm activity that can fully absorb you, which in turn will allow you to escape everyday hurdles for a while, and deeply relax. It's a great activity if you find yourself overwhelmed and negative thoughts start running through your mind.

4. Swimming

Swimming is a great exercise which allows you to focus on your breathing and rhythmical movements. It does not require a lot of effort; however, it can bring a deep relaxation to your while body afterwards. It relieves tension like nothing else and usually comes with minimal distractions. All you need is a body of water suitable for swimming.

5. Dancing

Dancing can truly be a therapeutic experience. It allows you to focus on expression and can help activate the healing processes of your body. When dancing you connect with your body on a different level, which allows you to express feelings that are often hard to convey with words. It is highly beneficial if you suffered trauma or have anxiety or depression.

You become mindful when you dance, which in turn allows you to learn more about yourself and your body. It expresses your creativity through the flow of pleasant physical sensations. You dissolve in the moment, and that is a truly healing experience.

Add mindful movement to your daily routine

Whatever practice you may choose, the most important thing is to focus your awareness on the present moment. Pay attention to the movement of your hands and feet, feel the surface you're standing on, feel the motion.

Focus on your breath as you inhale and exhale. Notice how the air travels into your nostrils and out. Allow the rhythmic movements to flow and relax your mind.

Be aware of your surroundings. Notice the sounds, smells and movement around you. Use your senses to ground yourself in the moment.

Examine your experiences, thoughts, and feelings without judgement. If you get lost in thoughts, shift back to the movement, return to the moment, to now.

Try to incorporate mindful movement into your daily routine. It will help you relax your mind and release stress and tension from your body. Include your favorite mindful activities into your everyday life and try to make it your habit.

Don't forget to use this technique when you're facing struggles or start getting overwhelmed. Return to a relaxed state and release any tension and stress that might have accumulated. It's a great way to overcome anxiety, restore your energy, and get back to your daily life feeling energized and ready to tackle anything in your way head-on.

As we've raised the topic of mindful movement, let's examine what mindfulness is in more detail and what practical benefits it can offer to improve your life.

Mindfulness

Mindfulness provides the ability to feel happy and content in any circumstances, despite any worries you might have. It also helps find a connection to something beyond our concerns. It brings an increased awareness of our connection to the others and our surroundings, which in turn provides a deeper understanding of your life, thus making us content.

If our minds are left undirected, they can make us anxious and unhappy in many different ways. Let's see how practicing mindfulness can improve your quality of life.

What is mindfulness?

Mindfulness fundamentally consists of three elements and is defined as paying attention in a particular way to these elements: on purpose, in the present moment, and without judgement. Once again, these are the three fundamental elements of mindfulness to keep in mind:

1) On purpose
2) In the present moment
3) Non-judgmental

Mindfulness can also be described as the skill of

knowing what's happening in your head at any given moment without getting carried away by it. Before we move on to how to actually practice mindfulness, let's take a look at what happens when we aren't mindful.

What happens when we aren't mindful

We've already touched on the idea that our minds can make us anxious and unhappy if left undirected. It doesn't mean our minds are flawed. Of course, they can be changed, rebuilt, developed and improved, otherwise nothing would make a difference, even practices like mindfulness. Our minds have qualities that we either fail to notice or choose to ignore, instead of managing them. These qualities are:

- Limited views of the world
- Bias towards negativity
- The role of subconsciousness in our daily lives

Without mindfulness we can get caught up in our thoughts and emotions, and become completely identified with them. We've talked about how this is an emotional response and does not necessarily represent the truth, yet we tend to forget about it and fall into this trap over and over again.

In fact, this works fine if we are having pleasant experiences, but of course that is not always the case. During times of anxiety and stress, this can lead to a vicious cycle of negative thoughts and crippling self-doubt. Practicing mindfulness helps you get out of your head and observe the situation more clearly.

How mindfulness helps us know our ego

It's become quite popular to talk about the ego lately; however, it's important to remember that ego in itself is not all bad. Ego is essentially the same as personality. Our personalities are shaped from an early age by our experiences with the world and other people. Beliefs play a big role in molding our personality or our ego.

As a result, most of us associate themselves with this ego. Consequently, you become completely identified with your personality. This is a problem, even if you are really nice and cute. You're probably wondering why this is a problem. It's only natural to associate ourselves with our personality or ego, isn't it? The problem is that it becomes inherently difficult to observe our ego when we associate ourselves with it.

Self-improvement depends on your ability to take a

look at yourself from the side - as an observer. Only when you're completely honest with yourself, you can identify the areas that need improvement. It is possible to step outside our ego, although for a brief moment, but that is usually more than enough.

Not only is it essential for self-improvement, but it is also a very relaxing experience. It gives us an opportunity to see ourselves apart from our egos, our true selves. This is the main reason why it is important to practice mindfulness.

The observing self

Mindfulness allows us to observe ourselves apart from our ego. Consequently, practicing mindfulness is related to cultivating the observing self in our daily lives and freeing our minds from limiting aspects.

Our ego is responsible for our thinking self. It is the part of the mind which operates your memories, thoughts, beliefs and judgements. Essentially, it's the ego.

The observing self is the part responsible for awareness of whatever you are thinking and doing at any given moment. Mindfulness helps you cultivate and operate from the viewpoint of the observing self.

Practicing mindfulness

The best thing about mindfulness is that you can practice it anytime and anywhere.

Considering you might be unfamiliar with the practice, it can be helpful to train your brain to do it by formalizing it. What it means is that you should allocate a certain time and activity that you will spend in a state of mindfulness. You can do it on a walk, on your commute or when doing house chores - it doesn't matter.

Many people who begin practicing mindfulness find using labeling quite useful to sort of "turn on" the observing self. Labeling allows you to drive a wedge between you and your thoughts. Essentially, you are simply labeling your thoughts and actions. For example, "I am thinking about my job now", "Feeling angry now", "Worrying about my kids", "I was blamed for something I didn't do". This is labeling and you can use it when you're just starting out practicing mindfulness.

Later on, you can try spending most of your day in a state of mindfulness. It will help you observe your thoughts instead of being in them, which is an incredibly relaxing experience.

The difference between mindfulness and meditation

It can seem like mindfulness is similar to meditation in some ways, and it is true to some extent. However, there is one major difference between the two practices.

During meditation our goal is to notice when we become distracted by thoughts, and switch our focus to something neutral, like our breath. When we practice mindfulness, we simply observe, we don't direct our attention to anything in particular.

Meditation can complement mindfulness, so you can look into starting meditating if you'd like. Even five minutes a day is enough.

How practicing mindfulness can help us cope with daily struggles

The benefits of mindfulness come from one simple fact. We are not our thoughts or emotions. We have the power of choice and we can choose to be calm and content with whatever might be going on. The main benefit of mindfulness is the ability to feel happy and content, regardless of what might be happening. Here are some more benefits you will achieve once you start practicing mindfulness:

1. The majority of our opinions are not useful

It's natural that we have opinions about pretty much everything that surrounds us and even ourselves. But what is their purpose? Have you ever wondered that?

Our opinions about ourselves are the product of our inner self-talk. Practicing mindfulness makes our inner self-talk more evident. We've established that our beliefs are formed by our inner self-talk, based on the external input we receive. Thus, it affects our self-confidence and the way we carry ourselves.

Regarding our opinions of others and the world around us - they usually don't hold the significance we attribute to them. In most cases, they tell more about ourselves than other people. When you have negative thoughts about a situation or other people, it usually means you're feeling stressed and tired. You can notice that when you practice mindfulness.

2. We are controlled by our attachments

Attachments have two forms - attractions and aversions. Attractions are, for example, friendly faces, sunny weather, or the smell of delicious food. Aversions include things like loud noises, being rejected, or disgusting coffee.

We are wired to avoid discomfort and pain and are attracted to pleasure. Our attachments to pleasant things can work against us and hinder our progress on the way to achieving bigger goals.

The opposite of attachment is, you guessed it, detachment. Detachment is a mindfulness practice that allows you to notice when you become agitated, and avoid getting caught up in the chase for attachments as a result. This way you can make attachments have less impact on your life.

3. We use specific reality buffers to filter reality

We tend to unconsciously use psychological defense mechanisms as emotional buffers to filter reality. It is possible to detect them once you start practicing mindfulness, and almost impossible to notice them otherwise.

Our mind uses psychological defense mechanisms to defend three areas of psychological concern, which are:

• Bearing need and dependency as an inevitable part of relationships

• Managing intense emotions

• Developing a sense of self-esteem

These are the specific psychological defense mechanisms that our mind uses to defend these areas of psychological concern:

- Repression and denial
- Displacement and reaction formation
- Blaming
- Splitting
- Idealisation
- Projection
- Control
- Thinking
- Narcissism

Now that you know these psychological defense mechanisms, you can recognize them in yourself. With time and practice, you will be able to train your mind to stop using them at all.

4. Responding in the moment

Mindfulness practice can show you when you are least present and how exactly. It can help you become aware of unhelpful habits. Pretty much everyone has a thing or things they do.

If you tend to get carried away, it can help you get

back in the moment. Mindfulness practice can reveal the obstacles to achieving satisfaction and feeling pleasure.

It's natural to expect practical benefits if you are going to start practicing something. In case of mindfulness, the main benefit is the ability to feel happy and content, no matter what is going on in your life. Mindfulness is one of the most practical things you can do to increase the quality of your life.

Another huge benefit of practicing mindfulness is the ability to cultivate the observing self. It will help you see yourself separately from your ego and personality, which in turn will allow you to see what areas need improvement. It will help you detach from your thoughts and emotions and see things more clearly. Living without the distortions of our mind is a relaxing experience. You should consider starting practicing mindfulness if you haven't already.

Responsibility

Responsibility is the ability to determine our response to any circumstances. It is the ultimate habit of people who possess high personal effectiveness. It gives you the feeling of real freedom that nobody and nothing can take away. Responsibility allows you to make the most important decision - to be proactive over your responses.

You are free from influence if you choose your response

Once again, it's important to remember we have the power of choice. Developing responsibility is your choice and a decision that you can make at any given moment. Keep in mind, we choose whether we allow others to hurt ourselves. Nobody and nothing can hurt us without our consent. Responsibility grants you this freedom to choose. It is the ultimate defense against the fear of failure, rejection and rapidly changing conditions.

By default, we usually choose to act reactively. Responsibility is all about acting proactively. Let's take a look at how we can move from reactivity, our default position, to proactivity in our responses.

What is the freedom to respond?

Everything is relative and quite often it's useful to remember that your situation is far better than the circumstances of a lot of people. Let's take a look at the prisoners in the death camps of Nazi Germany, for example.

Viktor Frankl was a Jewish psychiatrist, a holocaust survivor who lived through multiple Nazi death camps. He wrote a book "Man's Search for Meaning", where he described what he called "the last of human freedoms". It's related to the ability to decide how unimaginable horror can shape our identities.

Frankl established that despite the horrors he had to live through, his identity was still intact. He discovered the freedom to respond.

Many of us probably never experienced something even remotely close to what holocaust survivors had to live through. Despite that, we neglect to use our ability to choose what to focus on when we encounter unfair or poor treatment.

How taking responsibility can change your life

It's not hard to see why exercising responsibility can change your life. Imagine you had the ability to choose whether to be upset by bad news, such as being fired, or not. Or by your partner's behavior. Or by difficult people you have to deal with on a daily basis.

With responsibility, you can meet all of these scenarios with proactivity and action. It is one of the best decisions you can make.

Being responsible for your responses prevents a lot of stress and anxiety. When you realize you can choose your responses to various things, you will have a lot more confidence in taking actions to build your future and communicating how you feel. This will make you more focused and determined, as you will become more willing to face discomfort and will not be afraid of failure or rejection because you will be able to stop focusing on them.

You need a strong sense of value first

Before we move on to learning to choose your responses and practicing responsibility, there is one crucial thing we need to discuss first. Practicing responsibility requires the ability to put your emotional responses aside.

Let's imagine you have to work with someone who constantly interrupts you. It's natural to feel irritated, as we are born reactive. Irritation is a natural reaction in this case. However, it's more rational to work on a solution to the problem instead of displaying your irritation.

Being naturally reactive, we are driven by feelings

113

and emotional responses. Responsibility is all about being proactive, therefore we will be driven by our internal values. When you practice responsibility, your responses will be based on your values. That is why you have to examine your core values before you develop your ability to choose responses.

Learning to choose your response

Developing responsibility is fairly straightforward - all you have to do is make a decision. Of course, it's easier said than done, as you will need discipline and control. Here is a step-by-step guide on how to develop the habit of responsibility.

1. Listen to your language

The words we use reveal a lot of things. In particular, they show whether we consider ourselves either acting or acted upon. Reactive language removes responsibility, which can bring relief in the short term, but it works both ways.

Let's take a look at some common phrases and excuses:

- "It is just who I am"
- "I have to"

- "He makes me angry"

  You can change this to the following:

- "I can choose to change"

- "I choose to"

- "I can choose my feelings"

Responsibility gives you the power to choose anything - your feelings, how you react, and your actions. Proactivity allows you to generate feelings instead of waiting for them to happen.

2. Consider where you focus your time and energy

We have a circle of concern and a circle of influence. The circle of concern are the things we care about. The circle of influence are the things we have control over. When practicing responsibility, you focus your time and effort on your circle of influence.

This is why you have to consider where you focus your time and energy. Mindfulness can help you take a look at yourself from an observer standpoint, which will help you establish how you can refocus your time and efforts. It is easier said than done, of course, but with time and practice you will be able to establish what you can control and what truly maters to you.

3. Categorize the difficulties you have to face

We can divide the problems we encounter into three categories:

- Direct - problems connected with our own behavior
- Indirect - problems linked with other people's behavior
- No control - problems we can do nothing about

Being responsible and proactive, you can include all three types of problems in your circle of influence. "But wait, what about the problems we can do nothing about? How can I have control over those?" - you might wonder. Here are practical examples of how you can include all three types of problems into your circle of influence:

Imagine you have a direct problem that you spend too much time playing video games and not enough time on learning a new skill. This is easy - a proactive response would be to change your habits.

Let's take a look at an indirect problem. For instance, your colleague is slacking or otherwise behaving unprofessionally. This, in turn, affects your work. When you put this problem in your circle of influence, you will consider how you can change this situation or this person. There are many different strategies you could use. You can confront your colleague or influence your boss to assign someone else. The main thing is that you put your efforts into looking for a solution instead of pointlessly complaining about your colleague's behavior. You're actually taking action to change the situation instead of complaining and ruminating.

Now comes the most interesting part. What about the problems we have no control over? The answer is quite simple - this is where the practice of acceptance comes into play. In a few words, it means you accept the things you cannot change, which leaves you free to focus on the things you have control over. We will talk about acceptance really soon - in the upcoming part.

The role of mindfulness

Responsibility is best combined with mindfulness because it allows you to observe your true self and notice the space between stimulus and reaction. If you know what happens in that space, you will be able to choose your responses more effectively. Developing responsibility and practicing mindfulness are closely related.

117

The ability to choose your responses that comes with practicing responsibility is the ultimate skill that will transform your life. In addition to that, you'll learn how to view your problems and where to focus your time and energy. This will improve your personal effectiveness and nothing and nobody will be able to hurt you. Because now you can choose.

Acceptance

We've discovered how mindfulness combined with responsibility can help you vastly improve your life. There is one final practice to complete the ultimate toolkit - acceptance.

It might sound easy - just accept what you can't change, right? But it's hard to explain and learn how to do it in practice. In short, acceptance is about experiencing your feelings directly, without filtering or sorting them.

It's not just a cognitive process, some people neglect to notice it is actually a bodily process. Besides, technically we don't really learn acceptance. Instead, we unlearn our habit of non-acceptance.

So, let's take a look at what non-acceptance is and how it happens.

What is non-acceptance and how it happens

Most people divide their lives between wanted experiences, such as excitement and pleasure, and emotions they find uncomfortable or unpleasant. People tend to avoid things like sadness, loneliness, and boredom. Instead of accepting these feelings directly, we try to excessively rationalize them or totally reframe our experience by finding some sort of escape.

That is the reason why most don't see acceptance as a part of personal growth. However, if we continue not accepting our feelings directly and keep avoiding or escaping them, sooner or later we will find ourselves in a constant pointless chase for excitement and pleasures. You can probably notice how many people are afraid of letting their lives go quiet even for a moment, they can't slow down and feel it all.

It's highly likely you are selective with experiencing your feelings. Using mindfulness, try to take a look at yourself from an observer point of view and notice how you filter your feelings, emotions, and experiences. We are naturally drawn towards pleasure and excitement. Because of that, we have tons of unprocessed emotional experiences which we have filtered out. Avoiding a problem doesn't make it go away. You can't run from your true feelings forever. It leads us to severe anxiety and dysfunction.

But enough with that sad talk. Let's see what we can do to help ourselves experience our emotions directly. Let's discuss what it means to practice acceptance.

What does it mean to practice acceptance?

Despite the fact that "acceptance" sounds simple, it's difficult to explain the concept. We've established that, in short, acceptance is experiencing your emotions directly. However, if you simply tell yourself to experience your emotions directly, you will still apply thought process to that. Dropping out of the mind and experiencing emotions directly is not as easy as it might seem.

Furthermore, acceptance can get mistaken for giving up. This is not correct, as we will discuss later on. However, because of that association, most don't see acceptance as a part of personal growth.

Another misconception surrounding acceptance is confusing acceptance with accepting our personal circumstances. Accepting circumstances outside of your direct circle of influence is a good thing; however, it's important to understand this is related to responsibility, not acceptance.

Now that we know what acceptance is not, let's take a look at what is actually is.

Acceptance is the willingness and ability to experience ourselves and our lives as they are. It is a departure from self-deception towards reality.

What we don't accept

We easily accept positive emotions, such as excitement and validation. We tend to avoid and escape more depressive feelings, such as sadness, loneliness, disappointment, and despair. In addition to that, we often choose to ignore some feelings and traits in ourselves that we judge others for, such as laziness or being picky.

When we practice acceptance, we explore all our feelings with curiosity. We don't choose what to accept and what to filter out. We experience everything as is. In fact, we welcome harder emotions and explore them with interest and eagerness.

That might sound unreasonable and perhaps even mental or sadistic. However, it's important to remember there are consequences to not accepting our emotions. If we continue to neglect some of them, sooner or later we will

121

start having difficulties being able to embrace any of them. Non-acceptance makes us disconnected from ourselves, as we process reality through the filter of our neediness. Acceptance allows us to process all the emotions through our hearts and feelings and explore them to gain a deeper understanding of ourselves and the world.

How to establish what you don't accept

It seems like an easy question, but the answer won't be obvious. It's difficult to be completely honest with yourself and understand what you might subconsciously filter out. Mindfulness can help you discover what you don't accept and choose to ignore or avoid. It allows you to take a look at yourself from the point of view of an observer. This way it's much easier to notice the things you tend to avoid and how you do it.

Practicing acceptance makes you happier

Positive emotions can never be such powerful catalysts to growth as negative emotions. If you've ever lived through tough times or even suffered, you can look back and see how it helped you grow. Negative emotions help build our character and can actually be beneficial for improving our positive states, such as building self-confidence.

When I was heartbroken at the end of a relationship, I relaxed into a state of deep sadness. This experience changed me. I remembered that there were certain moments that I wasn't thinking about what exactly happened, yet I wasn't just numb. I was there, present to my sadness.

I became more compassionate to myself after that. This would never happen if I kept avoiding my feelings like before. This gave me freedom like nothing else. This freedom you get when you practice acceptance contributes to higher happiness over time.

Not having control over our behavior is one of the things that keeps us feeling unhappy and helpless. When we aren't accepting something, we tend to develop compulsive habits. That happens because avoiding and ignoring our emotions creates a strain. To release it, we tend to indulge in compulsive habits, which can be fairly innocent, such as biting your nails, or destructive, such as alcohol or substance abuse.

Practicing acceptance allows us to experience emotions directly and avoid creating extra strain on our mind and body. Which in turn prevents us from developing unhelpful compulsive habits and leads to higher happiness.

Acceptance prevents you from identifying with the things you aren't accepting

When we avoid certain feelings long enough, it can be easy to get consumed by them. Practicing acceptance helps you avoid becoming consumed by the feelings you've been avoiding.

Let's take a common trait, such as laziness, for example. We can judge ourselves for it, but ultimately, we try to ignore or avoid it. Experiencing laziness directly can sound like a total nonsense; however, this experience can be transformative.

When we stop resisting laziness, our identity as being lazy falls apart. This way we can unlock unstoppable energy that is usually blocked by our habit of avoiding or running away from our feelings. Without the pressure of our ego, we can gain a fresh outlook at ourselves. This is how laziness or any other habit can bring us to compassionate life.

When we stop resisting certain emotions, we stop being defined by them. When we stop struggling against laziness, we stop identifying so much with it. This can be applied to other emotions too, like sadness, loneliness, despair, and grief. If you welcome and accept them, then you stop identifying with them.

Three misconceptions surrounding acceptance

1) Does practicing acceptance mean resignation?

As mentioned previously, acceptance is not the same as resignation. When we resign, we give up and remain passive. On the contrary, when are willing to accept things, we demonstrate courage and show compassion to ourselves. Practicing acceptance leads to higher personal effectiveness and developing strengthening qualities. Acceptance makes change possible.

We are taught that looking down on ourselves negatively is how we improve. However, the best way to self-improvement is letting yourself feel what you need to feel. This way, you can establish what you need to do about it. This is how we develop emotional intelligence, which we will talk about in more detail in the next chapter.

2) Can we pass acceptance and just choose to

be positive?

Reframing negative experiences is perhaps the most common form of non-acceptance. We have to remember that we involve cognitive process every time we try to reframe our experiences. If we do it regularly, if we need to reframe in order to be okay with whatever is happening, it turns into a struggle.

Like most people, I have been reframing certain experiences too, so I wasn't held back by emotions that much. In fact, reframing can be quite effective and there is a time and place for it too. But we have to remember that everything is good in moderation. Reframing your experiences all the time just isn't healthy or useful.

You can positively reframe your experiences from time to time, but doing it all the time is not a sustainable strategy and ultimately becomes a form of struggle.

3) Does acceptance equal bathing in our emotions?

Acceptance doesn't mean bathing in our emotions all the time and drowning in melancholy. Acceptance is about compassion to yourself.

When we become consumed by emotions, we are being consumed by our interpretations of them, in fact.

When we experience our emotions directly with the help of acceptance, we don't apply thought process, thus any negative sensations or suffering doesn't last long. If you often get caught up in your emotions, practicing mindfulness in conjunction with acceptance can make a huge difference.

Exercises in acceptance

Even though acceptance is not a cognitive process, here are five acceptance practices to help you improve your understanding of acceptance.

1. Mindfulness meditation

Mindfulness meditation is the essential acceptance practice. It allows us to relate to our daily struggles and gain deep clarity.

Doing mindfulness meditation is quite simple. You begin by bringing attention to your breath. Breath is the primary anchor in mindfulness meditation. Take several deep breaths and return to normal breathing. Pay attention to it, but there is no need to control it.

Eventually, you will notice your mind wants to drift off into thoughts. Mindfulness meditation is all about recognizing when this happens. You can use labeling in a similar manner to when you start practicing mindfulness. You can simply remark "thinking", and return your focus to your breath. To sum up, here are the steps to mindfulness meditation:

- Breathing is used as an anchor - take a few deep breaths and return to normal breathing
- Notice when your mind starts drifting off into thoughts
- Mark this moment by labeling it "thinking"
- Switch your focus back to breathing

This will help you gain deeper clarity, as you will be able to control when your mind starts drifting off into thoughts, thus preventing unhelpful rumination.

2. Facing difficulties and naming what's true

This exercise is geared towards helping you gain a deeper understanding about a difficult situation in your life.

Imagine the situation that is currently challenging you. It can be pretty much anything, from a personal conflict to stress at work or financial pressure. Ask yourself how you feel about it and bring a receptive presence to your body. Receptive presence is a condition of being without judgment or agenda of our own. Pay attention to your body, especially your throat, chest and stomach.

After describing how you feel and naming your experience, ask yourself if it's true. If not, continue to inquire. If you get lost in thoughts, return attention to your body. You can use labeling in the background, but most of your attention should be focused on awareness and attending to your experience.

3. Acceptance of pain

This practice helps relax our resistance to unpleasant sensations.

First, you need to enter a relaxed state. Now scan through your body. Pay attention to any areas where you feel discomfort or pain. Now bring attention directly to the unpleasant sensations in that part of your body. See what happens when you begin to be present with this pain. Do you attempt to push the pain away or somehow block or cut it off? Do you feel fear?

Imagine your awareness as a soft space that surrounds the pain. Allow the pain and any unpleasant sensations to float in that space. Now bring more focused attention to the changing sensations. Notice how your experience changes. Do you feel aching, stabbing, burning, or throbbing? Explore these sensations with soft, non-

129

reactive attention.

4. Discover your deepest longing

This practice helps bring your desires into the light. Our desires can actually hold a lot of fear.

Enter a relaxed, comfortable state. Ask yourself what your heart longs for. Initially, your answer could be that you want more money, lose weight, be healthy, or find love. Ask again and listen carefully, noticing what spontaneously arises.

Go on like that for a few minutes. Ask the question and pay attention and accept everything. Your answer should become simpler and deeper as you go on. Be patient, with time you will be able to discover your deepest longing this way.

5. Being with fear

Please note this practice may not be useful if you suffered trauma.

It can be practiced any time you feel fear. To begin, enter a relaxed state. Now imagine the situation that fears you. Ask yourself what you're really afraid of and what the worst part of this situation is.

Your answer can be similar to a story. Pay attention to the sensations that arise in your body, so that this story can become a gateway to experiencing your feeling deeper and more fully. Using your breath will help you touch your fear. Pay attention to your throat, chest, and stomach. Notice how fear expresses itself in you.

Out of the three practices - mindfulness, responsibility, and acceptance - acceptance is probably the most difficult to master. Acceptance should flow from mindfulness practice, as it helps you lose your identification with your thoughts and establish what you might not be accepting. Acceptance helps you experience your feelings directly. It allows you to move from self-deception towards reality.

Changing your environment

Many of us think we are our own persons and refuse to believe that we are vulnerable to external pressure. Having such strong beliefs might seem like a good thing; however, we have to consider what impact our environment has on us. Our environment has an enormous sway over us. When we realize it, we can bend it to our advantage.

We always hear how the environment we grew up in shaped us into who we are today. The same principle applies now, in the present. Your environment can subconsciously influence you in many ways.

This influence is much stronger during the formative years in your childhood. But it's still there now. The difference is that now you can choose how to move forward. You're no longer a kid being dragged in a linear manner with little say or understanding. You're now an adult with responsibilities and decisions to make.

Of course, you can go with the flow and continue on the same linear path as your childhood, allowing your environment and everything happening around you to just be. However, by doing so, you become dependent on your environment because you are not willing to question its authority.

On the contrary, you can choose to shake things up. You can begin shaping an environment that works in your favor. You can start by questioning the comfortable order around you. If you are willing to assess your situation in an honest way, you can build the environment for your success.

"What environments are there for you to change exactly?" - you might wonder.

In this case, we are talking about something that

affects your life daily. There are two main areas to it: mental environment and physical environment. Let's begin with the mental environment.

Mental environment

First, let's establish what mental environment actually is. Mental environment is the sum of all societal influences on mental health. It usually includes your social circle - those around you, your friends, acquaintances and family.

Most of us live in a fantasy world where we expect family to care for us and all our friends to have our back. Unfortunately, this is not always the case.

Toxic relationships and friendships can affect your mental health. In this case, you cannot accept your environment the way it is. When you're surrounded by negativity, it infiltrates your brain and all areas of your life. We often neglect to notice this, but before we know it, we find ourselves complaining, blaming everyone, and developing negative traits.

With time, it keeps affecting you more and more. You move further away from being your true self. Bad company corrupts good character.

On the other hand, there are people who don't leave you feeling down. Such company is good for you and your mental health. They don't feed on your energy and make you feel determined, optimistic, and ambitious.

Finding such people is not easy and may seem like a difficult task at first. After all, how can you find friends when you don't even know them first, right? Once you begin looking for something that is meaningful to you, it will naturally gravitate towards you. Ask yourself what your core values are and you will learn exactly who you are - your true self. It's often hidden beneath the veil of environmental negativity.

Physical environment

Our physical environment can be split into two levels: the micro level and the macro level.

The micro level

The micro level of physical environment is the smaller and more immediate level. You can look around and see what's distracting you from your goals.

It may sound weird, but let's use chocolate as an example. I love it, but I don't possess the discipline when it comes to chocolate. I have chocolate at my desk when I'm

134

working. I have lots of chocolate everywhere at home - in the kitchen, in my room, in my desk, I have a chocolate cake in the fridge and I will eat it all. There it is, and now it's gone in a couple of minutes.

What I have to do is change the environment by removing the temptation. It's not chocolate's fault after all, it's mine. By removing the temptation, I am changing the environment. Which in turn leads to reduction of sugar and fat intake, which allows me to lose weight and improve my health and fitness. Of course, it's not necessary to completely remove it. Everything is good in moderation, and I can enjoy some chocolate as a treat once in a while. But I won't eat the whole pack.

At the micro level, you can change your surroundings. For example, keep your room tidy, move the furniture, paint the walls a pleasant color, or add more plants if you'd like. Whatever you feel can aid your success, you should do it.

The macro level

The macro level of physical environment is your surroundings on a wider scale, it's the area you live in.

Perhaps you find yourself in an area you don't enjoy or you feel you don't belong there. Maybe the people around you are not good for your mental health. You cannot be the person you want to be in such an environment. You have to switch up your life and move in order to unburden yourself from such weight.

Moving can be a transformative experience. Many people find moving away from where they grew up a life changing experience. The same place can be perfect for some of us, whereas others have to move and explore in order to find their place in the world.

If you're unhappy somewhere, you can consider moving in order to change your physical environment. Of course, it's not as easy as just getting up and moving. There are personal circumstances that may prevent us from doing so. But if you feel the need to move, start by looking for a way to make that happen. It can be very difficult, but it's so worth it in the end.

Everything around you is fluid

If you feel stuck, consider popping that comfortable bubble and changing your mental and physical environment. If you want something you've never had, you have to do something you've never done. We need to change in order to grow, and changing your environment is a transformative experience. If you change your environment for the better - you will see positive changes in your life. It is in your control and you will thank yourself for it later.

Accept discomfort

When you encounter any challenges, you have to become more than you were before in order to overcome them. You have to explore new perspectives, learn new skills, and expand your boundaries. In other words, you have to gain a deeper understanding in order to be able to overcome any obstacles you might face.

Of course, it all comes with a fair share of discomfort. But the key to success is in the things we tend to avoid. These are things that break us down and humble us. Difficulty helps us grow, comfort doesn't. If everything is good, we tend to become stagnant. If you want to achieve success, you have to stop avoiding what's hard. You have to constantly push yourself to improve and do things that push your limits. You will experience a lot of discomfort along the way, but that's what you have to embrace in order to achieve success and reach your full potential.

Learning to accept discomfort and being

comfortable with it is one of the most valuable skills you can possess. If you learn to accept discomfort - you can master pretty much anything.

Of course, staying with discomfort doesn't come naturally. But so don't many things. When we are born, we can't talk, walk, or even eat on our own. We learn to do it all as well as many other skills when we grow up. Constant self-improvement is the key to success. Finding ways to be comfortable with your discomfort is an essential skill for living the life you want. Personal development always involves the ability to accept and manage discomfort.

If you learn to accept discomfort - you can master pretty much anything

Discomfort is a part of personal growth. Accepting discomfort allows you to beat procrastination, which in turn opens up a vast amount of possibilities. You can start a new habit, learn a new language, try new things, simplify your life, and overcome any challenges you face.

These tasks may seem quite daunting at first, but when you learn to accept discomfort, you'll be able to do pretty much anything with eagerness and ease.

Think about the things that were uncomfortable for

you once, but which you accept now without effort. If you practice things that bring you discomfort enough, your comfort zone will expand to accept discomfort. Repetition expands your comfort boundaries.

Many of us avoid discomfort. Some people do everything they can to avoid discomfort. This can become the biggest limiting factor for most people. If you're too comfortable and cannot be bothered to make a change to improve your life, you will be bound to stay stuck in a stagnant state.

When you constantly avoid discomfort you restrict yourself to a rather small comfort zone. Consequently, it makes you miss out on most of life. Most of the best things in life, in fact.

Let's take a look at a practical example. Most people consider eating healthy food and exercising difficult and uncomfortable. Consequently, you turn to comfort foods and start leading an inactive lifestyle, which makes you unhealthy as a result. Being unhealthy is also uncomfortable, which makes you seek distractions, such as more unhealthy food, entertainment and shopping, which in turn makes things far worse. It can become a vicious, never-ending cycle.

However, if you simply can accept discomfort, it solves all of these problems. This is why it's important to learn to accept discomfort.

How to accept discomfort

Learning to accept discomfort is one the best skills you can learn, as your life will have almost no limits. Here are the steps you should take in order to learn to accept discomfort.

1. Try it in small doses in the beginning

Initially, try accepting discomfort in small doses. Stay for 30 seconds in an uncomfortable situation. Let's say you dislike exercising. Do some simple physical exercises for 30 seconds. You probably won't like it much at first, but with time you can even build a routine. For instance, getting up every hour to do 5-10 minutes of simple exercises or stretching.

2. Immerse yourself in discomfort

You probably sometimes feel angry, stressed, sad, or frustrated. It's okay, it's a part of human experience after all. However, as mentioned previously, we tend to avoid negative emotions and feelings. Use your power of acceptance to embrace and dive into these emotions. Or, let's say, you're experiencing procrastination from time to time. In this case, stop running away from the task at hand and sit down with it, don't switch to anything else. Yes, it might be uncomfortable at first, but you'll get used to it.

3. Seek discomfort

That might sound a bit extreme, but you have to do something in order to master it. In order to learn to accept discomfort, you have to seek it. Find things you find uncomfortable and do them. Put yourself up to the challenge every day. It can be anything: go for a run, confront someone, say no to people, hug a friend, try new things.

4. Notice how you run away from things

Consider the things you've been avoiding because of discomfort. Think of the experiences and feelings you've been rejecting. Think why you've been rationalizing and what problems are arising from discomfort. Become aware of the things you've been avoiding due to discomfort and see if you can stop running away from them, one by one.

You shouldn't fear discomfort. Discomfort is a natural part of self-improvement. When you're uncomfortable, you're learning something new, you're expanding your capabilities, you're becoming more than you were before. Discomfort is a sign you're growing.

Discomfort is a catalyst for personal growth

Personal growth depends on new challenges as you learn how to overcome them. Our mind is like a muscle that grows when it's worked upon. Without that work, muscles shrink, and so do our minds when we indulge ourselves in comfort. We have to tackle the fear that prevents us from reaching our goals. Your mind has a way of rising to the occasion. Challenge it constantly and it will reward in ways you could never imagine.

Many things seem impossible until they are done. You have to challenge your mind even by making it a little uncomfortable by making yourself learn things that may not come naturally. Give yourself permission to expand your boundaries and think beyond the usual.

Good things in life take time to mature - wine, works of art, or a healthy financial portfolio, for example. You can reach the best life ahead of you with patience, determination, diligence, and strategic action. You are the only one who can push yourself further.

Most of us think that if they had every comfort available to them, they'd be happy. We associate happiness with comfort. And now we've become so comfortable we're miserable. We have no struggle in our lives, no sense of adventure. We drive comfortable cars, we get in an elevator - everything comes easy. We are never more alive than when we're pushing and struggling for high achievements through all the pain and suffering that comes with it. That struggle is where the magic happens.

Practice even when it hurts

You have to keep challenging yourself and pushing beyond your limits. Unfortunately, most of the time we can be inconsistent. Even if you make an action plan and stick to it, there will be times you'll feel like giving up. That will probably never go away. But the ultimate goal should keep you motivated enough to keep pushing through all the hardships. Your progress should be your ultimate motivation. Pushing forward when something it annoying or painful builds character. Keep challenging yourself and you will be able to overcome any obstacle on your way to achieving things that matter to you.

CHAPTER 5: Mastering the power of long-term thinking and emotional intelligence

Long-term thinking

We find it easier to obsess over setbacks in the moment than try and play the long game. Of course, the obstacles are real and are right in front of you, while the future is far away and nothing is promised to no one.

Disappointments can easily overwhelm us, but we have to remember they are just a part of our lives. The key to success is to constantly move forward and not become caught up in our troubles for too long.

Henry Ford famously said: "When everything seems to be going against you, remember that the airplane takes off against the wind, not with it". We must not allow temporary setbacks to overpower our long-term plans.

Obstacles we face provide us with an opportunity to learn, if we are willing to look hard enough. Once the initial anxiety goes away, we can find ways to overcome setbacks and learn in the process.

We have to look at our lives as a whole, not just our failures. Some of us may be lucky and will live a long life. Regardless, we must not give our setbacks too much attention, since we will eventually bounce back from them one way or another.

We have an inherent bias towards negativity, which can get the better of us sometimes. The setbacks may be real, but we find ways to overcome them to the best of our ability. We have to switch our attention from negativity to the long-term view. There is a lot happening behind the scenes that we are not aware of. We have to learn our lessons from overcoming setbacks and constantly move forward towards our goals.

Discipline and self-control

The aim of developing a long-term view is not focusing on things in the moment, because ultimately you will either find a way to resolve them, or they will resolve themselves. You have to create a clear image of your proposed future instead of focusing on temporary setbacks.

Obstacles are a part of our lives. They may be difficult to overcome, but they are what allows personal growth on your way to success. In order to think long-term,

145

you have to adopt discipline and self-control.

The future is not promised and nobody knows what the future holds. But if you have a clear vision of what your future looks like, you can overcome short-term setbacks and pain that comes with them.

Obstacles, setbacks, failures, even bad luck and disasters are there to teach you, not hold you back. They make you improve, ultimately making you tougher. Anxiety and frustration are the fuel for personal growth. They give you the reason to toughen up and get organized, fix what you can, and move forward.

Long-term thinking allows you to realize you are never stuck in your present circumstances and that your situation will improve. Life constantly puts your inner resolve and strength to the test. This is how personal growth occurs, after all.

It might be difficult to adopt long-term thinking because we are not used to thinking far ahead. We are accustomed to dealing with the present situation and usually we have a limited view of tomorrow, not to mention the future.

Focusing on the current setbacks too much is unhealthy and can lead to crippling anxiety. Adopting long-term thinking allows you to focus on the bigger goals and avoid getting stuck in the present circumstances. Let's see how we can develop the long-term thinking mindset.

Imagine your proposed future

Long-term thinking is essentially visualizing your future through the power of imagination. At the beginning, you can focus on smaller destinations rather than larger goals.

The most important thing you have to remember is that you have to take action, no matter how small. You can do it through self-reinforcement, visualization, and affirmations. Success is built on the smallest details.

Your perception of time affects every part of your life. If you indulge in dwelling on the past, it becomes difficult to appreciate the present moment and plan your future.

Here's how long-term thinking works in practice. Let's say, your goal is to lose 10 kilograms, or 22 pounds, in 6 months. But there is a setback - you've suffered an injury. Naturally, it will make it difficult, if not impossible, to exercise and reach your goal. However, instead of focusing on the setback, you can consider alternative solutions that

147

will help you adhere to your goal.

You can use this time to work on your nutrition. Create a caloric deficit, while introducing more protein-rich and healthy foods into your diet. You will lose weight and adopt a habit of eating a healthy diet at the same time. Yes, it will take more time, but by the time you can exercise again you will lose some weight and adopt a healthy diet, which will make it much easier to lose more weight and become more fit and healthy.

You have to change your inner self-talk in order to stop focusing on the setbacks and start looking for alternative solutions. This skill will totally change your life and help you overcome any setbacks you might face.

Make a detailed picture of your life at some point in the future every month or two

Now that you've learnt how to start adopting long-term thinking, let's move on to setting concrete long-term goals that will be your guideposts on your way to success.

Imagine how you want your life to realistically look like in five years. Now think about ten years. And twenty years. It sounds easy, and many of us can daydream about it quite often. But the difference between daydreaming and

148

long-term thinking is that you have to sit down and make a detailed sketch of your future life. It will give you a realistic but positive vision of the future that you've planned for yourself, rather than random happy glimpses of what might happen.

The best way to do it is to dedicate an hour every month or two. First, choose a time frame - five, ten, or twenty years. Then go through different areas of your life and establish how you want things to look in this area. You can ask yourself the following questions:

• Health and body: How healthy is my body? Am I reasonably fit for my age? How have I improved my health?

• Intellectual: What have I learnt? What skills have I mastered? What new ideas have I explored?

• Spirituality: Have I become more mindful? What insight have I gained into the purpose of my life?

• Marriage and family: How is my relationship with my partner? How is my family life?

• Parenting: How are my kids growing up? How is my relationship with my kids? Did it develop into a healthy relationship between adults?

• Social: How are my relationships with my friends? Do I have strong relationships with them?

• Career: How is my career developing, what have I done to improve my career? What did I achieve? Did I successfully retire?

• Finance: Do I have financial security? What have I done to improve my financial situation? Can I retire?

• Other areas: What other significant initiatives have I started? Is there anything else I want to consider in my life?

Think about all these questions and anything related to them and come up with concrete answer for how you'd like your life to look like in that area. Your vision should be positive but realistic. Consider things you can realistically achieve.

From there, start making plans for the near future. Think what you need to do to make that happen.

You should write it all down. Take a notebook, write down questions and your answers and any thoughts that might pop up along the way. Make a plan based on your positive but realistic vision of your future.

It is a fairly simple process, and it makes your mind

used to naturally thinking about your future in realistic detail. With time and practice, it becomes a natural type of thinking.

At the beginning of each day, think of one significant thing you can do today that will make your life better a year from now and make that a top priority

I've been doing this for quite a while now. Every morning when I wake up, I think what I could do today outside of my normal routine that would provide some sort of benefits in at least a year. You can look at this like seeds for the future. Here are some examples:

1) Help someone run some errands
2) When you see someone struggle, offer help or at least just listen
3) Help someone move
4) Sign up for volunteer work
5) Take care of someone's child or pet when they are really busy or in an emergency
6) Call someone close to you and talk about them entirely. Listen and ask questions about them instead of talking about yourself or your feelings.

7) Offer to help someone or review their work before they have to submit it

8) Take over household chores if someone is really busy or having an emergency

9) Check in on someone who you know is struggling

10) Give a positive reference about someone else

I did all of that with no expectation of anything in return. It turned out it had a positive effect on my life in all areas - personal, professional, financial, and spiritual. Which in turn made me put more effort into planting these seeds every day.

Keep your eyes for spontaneous opportunities throughout the day to do such things. Think what you can do to make the future better. Don't worry about what you might get in return. Just do it and assume that good things will come your way eventually as a result.

Make the things you enjoy in the short term match up with your long-term goals

Simply speaking, try to make as many things you do on a daily basis align with your bigger long-term goals.

Let's say, you want to improve your finances, but you are guilty of spending money in unnecessary ways. In that case, you should find enjoyable daily routines that will make you switch your focus away from spending. Start changing your daily routine and try to avoid situations where you might spend money unnecessarily. Change your habits and find other things to do to fill the time when you would spend money uncontrollably.

One way to do it is changing your daily commute. If you like drinking coffee, you can start making it at home. Enjoy a cup of coffee at home and take one with you in a thermos cup instead of hitting a coffee shop. There are a lot of little joys, but you can find alternative ways to enjoy them cheaper or find less expensive replacements.

Let's take a look at another example. You want to get in better shape, but you don't really exercise and your lifestyle is mostly sedentary. In this situation, you could find some activities that you enjoy and just do them.

Try new things: go for a walk, do some gardening, join a fitness class, or, if you're feeling adventurous, a martial arts class. Try new things until you find something you enjoy and stick with it, make it a part of your daily routine.

This approach works with any part of your life.

Create a caloric deficit and start eating healthier

foods if you'd like to lose some weight. If you want to advance your career, dedicate some time every day to doing something that expands your abilities and improves your skills.

To sum up, find things you enjoy to fill your day that also have long-term benefits and help you reach your bigger goals.

Dedicate some spare time to think about specific elements of your future

You should find some time to reflect on your life and think about specific goals for your future.

Reflecting on your life is a sort of an after action review. Think about something you did recently and evaluate whether it was the best thing to do, what you could have done better, or perhaps there were more relevant things you should have done. Then think about specific elements of your future, how you want your life to look and how you can get there.

Let's take some specific goal as an example. Let's say, you want to buy a house in 10 years. That is a genuine goal, and of course you want it to be a real thing, one that doesn't damage your finances. Think how you can make it happen.

Should you start saving now? Should you take an extra project to save some money for the down payment? How big and expensive should your house be? What about the area? Maybe getting a smaller house or in a slightly more remote area is actually not such a bad idea?

Think about the concrete details and figure out what's feasible and what isn't. Establish what you have to start doing now to make it happen.

Focus on long-term goals

The main idea of the long-term thinking mindset is that there is always an action, no matter how small, that you can take that will bring you closer to your bigger long-term goals.

There will be obstacles and setbacks on the way. But with the skills you've learned, such as acceptance, responsibility, and mindfulness, you will not allow temporary setbacks to consume you. On the contrary, you will learn from them and move forward with determination and full of energy. Recognize setbacks as a minor process in a greater plan unfolding. This way you can use your setbacks as stepping stones for future success.

Deal with what is happening and use the lessons learned to focus on the bigger long-term goals. After all, this is where the result of your efforts lies. You should aim to seize it instead of dwelling on your past mistakes.

Now that you've learnt how to adopt long-term thinking, let's move on to the last piece of the puzzle - emotional intelligence. Developing your emotional intelligence will help you win the emotional game. You will learn how to control your emotions and choose your emotional responses in order to make appropriate decisions to reach the best outcomes.

Emotional intelligence

There are three main categories of capabilities responsible for a person's outstanding performance.

The first of these categories is technical skills. These are knowledge-based skills in different areas where we are operating. It's law for lawyers, accounting for accountants, psychics and math for engineers, history for historians, and so on.

The second category is cognitive abilities. These are brain-based skills which allow us to compete different tasks, from the simplest ones to the most complex. They are related to the process of learning, remembering, and problem-solving, rather than actual knowledge. These abilities include perception, recognition, and interpretation of sensory stimuli, as well as attention and the ability to sustain concentration on certain things in order to manage the demands in changing environments. Some practical examples of such abilities are memory, visual processing, language, and motor skills.

The third category is emotional intelligence. This is a group of skills which help maximize your own performance and the performance of those around you. The fundamental parts of emotional intelligence are self-awareness, self-regulation, motivation, empathy, and social skills.

In many cases, emotional intelligence is more important than intelligence or IQ when it comes to reaching goals in career or life in general. Nowadays our professional success mainly depends on our perception of other people's signals and reacting to them in an appropriate manner.

Thus, it's essential to develop your emotional intelligence in order to better understand, empathize, and negotiate with other people, especially today, as the economy is becoming more global.

Developing emotional intelligence can improve your understanding of yourself and others, it can help raise your awareness of your circumstances, and improve your ability to act in your own best interests and the best interests of people around you. Understanding your emotional data with the help of emotional intelligence will help you gain a better understanding of yourself and allow you to modify your internal self-talk.

Overcoming limiting beliefs is not easy for most of us, as we had a lifetime to develop and act on them. In addition to that, such beliefs are hidden from us because we accept them as the truth. We've learned how to overcome limiting beliefs and what long-term strategies we can employ to maintain our newly found fundamental beliefs. Emotional intelligence is an important trait that will help you master the emotional game. This, in turn, will help you act on your newly found fundamental beliefs and act in your own best interest and the best interest of those around you in the long run.

Five categories of emotional intelligence

The five categories of emotional intelligence are self-awareness, self-regulation, motivation, empathy, and social skills. Let's examine them in more detail:

1. Self-awareness

Self-awareness is the key to emotional intelligence. It is the ability to recognize an emotion as it happens. In order to develop self-awareness, you have to be completely honest with yourself and tune in to your true feelings. If you are able to recognize and evaluate your emotions, you can control them. Self-awareness consists of two major elements:

- Emotional awareness, which is your ability to recognize your emotions and their effects
- Self-confidence, which is your belief in your capabilities

2. Self-regulation

We have little control over when we experience emotions. However, it is possible to change how long an emotion will last by using certain techniques to clear yourself of negative emotions, such as anxiety, depression, or anger. We've talked about these techniques previously. They are reframing a situation in a more positive manner, taking a long mindful walk, or practicing mindfulness meditation. Self-regulation involves the following aspects:

- Self-control, which helps manage disruptive impulses
- Trustworthiness, which allows us to maintain honesty and integrity
- Conscientiousness, which is taking responsibility for our actions and their consequences
- Adaptability, which helps us adapt to the constantly changing environment
- Innovation, which in this case means being open to new ideas and trying new things

3. Motivation

In order to motivate yourself, you need to have clear goals and a positive mindset. Even though we are naturally biased towards negative attitude, you can learn to adopt a more positive mindset with time and effort. Reframing your thoughts in a more positive light can help in certain situations, but using this technique constantly is not healthy, as we've discussed previously. Ultimately, practicing acceptance can help you deal with negative emotions and keep moving forward towards your goals.

Motivation consists of the following elements:

- Achievement drive - your desire to constantly

improve in order to reach your goals or certain standards of performance

- Commitment - aligning with the goals of a group or an organization

- Initiative - readiness to act on opportunities

- Optimism - keeping pursuing your goals despite any obstacles or setbacks

4. Empathy

Empathy is the ability to recognize how other people feel. This is an important skill that will help you succeed in your life and career. Empathy allows you to recognize and understand the feelings others try to convey through certain signals. Which in turn allows you to control the signals you send to them.

Empathy helps us with:

- Service orientation - recognizing and meeting the clients' needs

- Understanding others - recognizing and understanding the feelings of others

- Developing others - recognizing where others need to improve and helping them to do it

5. Social skills

Nowadays having great interpersonal skills is necessary to succeed in your life and career. In the modern always-connected online world everyone has access to various knowledge. Consequently, people skills are even more important now than ever. You need a highly developed emotional intelligence to better understand, empathize, and negotiate with others in the modern global economy.

Here are the most useful social skills:

- Influence - using effective persuasion techniques
- Communication - conveying clear messages
- Leadership - inspiring and guiding others
- Change catalyst - initiating and managing change
- Conflict management - understanding, managing, and resolving conflicts
- Building bonds - creating and maintaining instrumental relationships
- Collaboration and cooperation - working with others towards a common goal
- Team capabilities - managing teams in pursue of common goals

Develop your emotional intelligence

Here is a step-by-step guide to developing and improving your emotional intelligence:

1. Identify and label your feelings

There are some feelings from which all others derive and evolve. They are fear, anger, sadness, disgust, shame, surprise, love, and enjoyment. For example, we can experience anxiety and nervousness from fear. We can feel hostility, resentment, and indignation from anger. Many emotions arise from sadness, such as melancholy, grief, sorrow, and self-pity. On a more positive side, we can feel joy, satisfaction, and relief from enjoyment. Love gives birth to adoration, acceptance, kindness, and friendliness. The list is long. What's important is recognizing your emotions and putting a name on them according to how you react to each of them. The first step to increasing your performance and personal effectiveness is recognizing and labeling your feelings. This way, you will know what you're working with in the first place.

2. Asses the intensity and duration of your feelings

Our emotions vary greatly in intensity and duration. Every feeling has its distinctive features. They have unique

163

psychological states and manifest themselves in different forms, intensities, and durations. They can range from a slight agitation or disturbance to psychopathologies that require professional attention and treatment.

Basic feelings have an emotional base at its core. There are moods surrounding it which are more muted, but last longer than the emotion itself. Beyond moods we can find temperament, which is essentially the readiness to evoke certain emotions or moods in response to stimulus. And further beyond that are disorders and clinical pathologies.

Assessing the intensity and duration of your emotions is the logical next step after identifying and labeling them, in order to gain a better understanding of your emotional life. This, in turn, will allow you to identify any disturbances that are characterized by unusually strong and long or weak and short emotions display.

3. Examine how you express emotions

Emotions consist of three main components: subjective, physiological, and expressive. Subjective component determines the way we experience our emotions personally. Physiological component defines how our bodies react to certain emotions. And finally, expressive component is responsible for our behavior and reaction in response to different emotions.

The expressive component plays an important role as it is responsible for the management of our emotions. In turn, it determines our positive and appropriate communication of our emotions.

4. Control your impulses

We've established that positive emotional management is important in every aspect of our daily lives. Strong willpower is the cornerstone of positive emotional management. Fortifying your willpower helps strengthen your character and provides better control of your emotions.

Controlling your impulses is the key to positive emotional management. We should not allow our impulses to control us and determine the outcome of our actions. Instead, we should control our impulses and drive them to the consecution of our desired outcomes. This will help you gain a sense of responsibility for your own life and allow you to effectively reach your goals.

Some simple examples of controlling your impulses is counting to three before answering a toxic person or letting the other person finish talking before jumping to conclusions. These are small actions that you can start doing daily. While they may seem small, mastering control of your impulses with these simple actions helps you massively improve your emotional intelligence in the long run.

5. Delay gratification

Delaying gratification is closely connected to controlling our impulses and strengthening willpower. This is considered to be one of the most effective traits of successful people. Delaying gratification is linked to long-term thinking, and it allows us to focus on the long-term perspective and build a sustainable approach to reaching bigger long-term goals. Of course, choosing to have something now may feel good in the short-term, but having discipline, managing impulses, and having strong willpower can result in bigger and better rewards in the future.

6. Reduce stress

Stress affects all areas of our lives. It has a significant negative effect on our social skills, which in turn leads to less successful communication.

When we are stressed, we tend to display negative non-verbal signals and, in the worst-case scenario, we can lose control over our emotions altogether. Reducing stress and creating a calm environment is an important step on the way to mastering your feelings and emotions.

7. Remember the difference between feelings and actions

Our emotions develop in two stages. During the first stage, our emotions grow and develop over time with increasing intensity. During the second stage, they fade away and how fast they disappear depends on the duration of the emotion.

Emotional intelligence is the skill that allows you to master your emotions. With emotional intelligence, you can use them at the appropriate time and the right way. In order to master emotional intelligence, we have to understand the difference between what we feel and what we do.

We have to understand that our brain uses emotions as mechanisms for survival. We feel fear to hide, anger to destroy our enemies, and sexual excitement to reproduce. However, with time and evolution, our brain has been forming the neocortex and developed an ability to create more complex strategies and plan long-term. Thanks to that, now we feel fear and no longer instinctively feel the need to hide, instead, we can use it to become better prepared. This is why we are able to control our anger and focus on the long-term goals, instead of momentary negative impulses. That is the reason we can feel sexual attraction and transform it into long-lasting family ties and love. Our intelligence and willpower allow us to choose our emotions and take appropriate decisions in order to reach the best outcomes.

Conclusion

In conclusion, let's summarize what we've learned about the power of belief, identifying and overcoming limiting beliefs, and the valuable strategies that will help you not only maintain your newly found fundamental beliefs, but also succeed in your life and career.

Belief is the conviction that something is true. However, most beliefs are formed in the absence of evidence. It's important to remember that beliefs are not a guide to the truth. The purpose of belief is to guide action, not to indicate truth. This is why one person is able to believe in their goals and take action to achieve them, while others are overwhelmed by self-doubt and have no power to press forward.

Your reality is created by your beliefs, so consequently you are creating our own luck, happiness, and everything else. Your brain matches the information it receives to the beliefs you have. What doesn't fit is simply discarded. This is why it's important to adopt and maintain fundamental empowering beliefs.

Our beliefs are formed from an early age. Most beliefs are formed during childhood. Unfortunately, not all

169

of us had great supportive parents and teachers. As a result, most of us have formed various limiting beliefs during our formative years. These limiting beliefs can greatly inhibit our abilities during the adult life.

However, if we adopted those limiting beliefs, it means we can adopt new fundamental beliefs to replace them. First, you need to establish which beliefs you have in general. You can do that by writing down all of your beliefs.

Then, you have to establish which beliefs are limiting you and which ones are helpful, so you can keep them. When examining your beliefs, keep in mind how useful a belief is in your particular situation in relation to the goals that you are trying to achieve. If it assists and supports you in reaching those goals - then keep it. But if it doesn't help and hinders your progress - this is obviously a clear sign that you are dealing with a limiting belief.

At this point, it's important to remember your beliefs are not the truth. Remember that your limiting beliefs are assumptions you make about reality that are not necessarily true.

To overcome your limiting beliefs, first make a list of beliefs that have held you back. Now take one of your beliefs and think of a time when it wasn't true. Examine how this belief has held you back. Try to remember when you first adopted this belief. Now think of the benefits you might have gained from this limiting belief. Sometimes limiting beliefs can have a purpose.

Finally, visualize getting rid of this belief. Imagine it as a wooden tablet that you throw far into the ocean with immense force and it disappears over the horizon. Now think of a statement opposite to that belief, write it down, and say it out loud. This is your new fundamental empowering belief. Now repeat this process for all your limiting beliefs.

Your newly found fundamental beliefs have to be maintained. As a quick fix, if you find yourself dwelling on negative thoughts, try to shift your negative self-talk into the past tense. For sustaining them long-term, there are certain techniques that we will reiterate now.

The first step to building self-confidence is facing your fears. It's important to keep in mind that if something feels scary, it doesn't necessarily mean that it's risky. You can overcome your fears by educating yourself on what risks are actually involved when doing things that scare you. Then you can create an action plan on how to approach overcoming your fears step by step. Another thing you can do is challenge your thoughts that don't necessarily make sense. Facing your fears is a great way to reduce anxiety and build more self-confidence.

Get moving to calm your body and mind. This will help you relax and release the tension. Introduce some mindful rhythmic movement routines into your daily life. It can be anything: walking, jogging, gardening, Hatha Yoga, or swimming. Considering that anxiety is the result of feeling stuck in our thoughts being unable to resolve something, rhythmic movement will help you get out of your head. Rhythmic movement improves your mood, reduces emotional stress and inflammation, and enhances your immune system. It makes you more relaxed, focused, and increases the feeling of security. It's exactly what we need in our daily struggles.

Next are the big three: mindfulness, responsibility, and acceptance.

If our minds are left undirected, they can make us anxious and unhappy in many different ways. Mindfulness provides the ability to feel happy and content in any circumstances, despite any worries you might have. It also helps find a connection to something beyond our concerns. It brings an increased awareness of our connection to the others and our surroundings, which in turn provides a deeper understanding of your life, thus making us content. Another huge benefit of practicing mindfulness is the ability to cultivate the observing self. It will help you see yourself separately from your ego and personality, which in turn will allow you to see what areas need improvement. It will help you detach from your thoughts and emotions and see things more clearly.

Responsibility is the ability to determine your response to any circumstances. It is the ultimate habit of a person who possesses high personal effectiveness. It gives you the feeling of real freedom that nobody and nothing can take away. Responsibility allows you to make the most important decision - to be proactive over your responses. It will help you learn how to approach any problems you might face and where to focus your time and energy.

Acceptance is the process of experiencing your feelings directly, without filtering or sorting them. Acceptance is the willingness and ability to experience yourself and your life as is. Acceptance should flow from mindfulness practice, as it helps you lose your identification with your thoughts and establish what you might not be accepting. Acceptance allows you to be content with

173

anything you can't change. It allows you to move from self-deception towards reality.

Remember, your environment can subconsciously influence you in many ways. We always hear how the environment we grew up in shaped us into who we are today. The same principle applies now, in the present. If you feel stuck, you should consider changing your mental and physical environment. Change your social circle. End your toxic relationships and friendships. See how you can change your physical environment at the micro level. Change up your living space. If you can, consider the possibility of moving altogether. You need to change in order to grow, and changing your environment is a transformative experience. If you change your environment for the better - you will see positive changes in your life.

Our daily lives are full of discomfort. But the key to success is in the things we tend to avoid. When you encounter any challenges, you have to become more than you were before in order to overcome them. Naturally, this may cause a fair share of discomfort. Learning to accept discomfort and being comfortable with it is one of the most valuable skills you can possess. If you learn to accept discomfort - you can master pretty much anything.

Now that we've learned the techniques and strategies to improve our daily lives and maintain fundamental beliefs, let's focus on the long-term goals. Adopting the long-term thinking mindset is crucial to succeeding in your life and career. Long-term thinking allows you to focus on your larger long-term goals instead of getting stuck in the moment and obsessing over setbacks. Furthermore, it will help you make the things you enjoy in the short-term match up with your long-term goals. The main idea of the long-term thinking mindset is that there is always an action, no matter how small, that you can take that will bring you closer to your bigger long-term goals.

Finally, developing your emotional intelligence will help you master your emotions and use them to your advantage. Developing emotional intelligence can improve your understanding of yourself and others, it can help raise your awareness of your circumstances, and improve your ability to act in your own best interests and the best interests of people around you.

Constant self-improvement is the key to success. Remember to examine your beliefs from time to time. You may find you've adopted some new limiting or negative beliefs, and that's okay. You can always take the necessary steps to replace them with empowering beliefs.

Don't forget your new fundamental beliefs need maintenance. React in the moment by shifting your negative self-talk into the past tense.

Use mindfulness to take a look at yourself from the point of view of an observer. Determine which areas of your life need improvement and work on them.

Introduce a mindful rhythmic movement routine into your daily life to release the accumulated tension, calm your body and mind, and keep staying relaxed.

Focus on the long-term goals with the power of long-term thinking. Don't allow temporary setbacks to throw you off course.

Any time you feel demotivated, come and read this book again. We tend to neglect and forget the most useful and important instruments we possess. This book contains all the tools you need to overcome self-doubt, boost your self-confidence, and succeed in your life and career.